SWIPED

SWIPED

How to Protect Yourself in a World Full of Scammers, Phishers, and Identity Thieves

ADAM LEVIN

with Beau Friedlander

PUBLICAFFAIRS
New York

Book design by Milenda Nan Ok Lee

Library of Congress Control Number: 2015912904
ISBN 978-1-61039-587-8 (HC)
ISBN 978-1-61039-588-5 (EB)

First Edition
10 9 8 7 6 5 4 3 2 1

To Heather and Jayger Wilde

Contents

PART 1
An Overview of the Problem

1

What's in a Name (and a Number)?

"I was just doing it to tease her, basically."

It was a harmless tweet. A girl named Brooklyn from Prosper, Texas, sent a picture to her friend Alanna in reply to one of many tweets about a cute boy Alanna had seen while shopping at a big-box store in nearby Frisco. Then something fundamentally unknowable happened: the mysterious Internet phenomenon of going viral.

Viruses reproduce by sending their DNA into a host cell, leaving the infected host, now itself a virus, to find another host cell for further reproduction. On the Internet, that process of cellular invasions and osmosis happens to users rather than cells, and it happens very fast. The DNA can be anything—a hilarious video or an unexpected quip harnessed to a snapshot. On November 2, 2014, the DNA was Brooklyn Reiff's week-old picture of a teenage boy named Alex Lee, tweeted as a playful fillip to her friend's obsession.

How did Brooklyn's sneaky shot of Alex Lee invade an entire population, replicating her friend Alanna Page's crush in one user after another?

You might call it theft. In fact, there were a lot of little robberies— and they added up. The first one happened when Brooklyn went beyond the act of stealing a glimpse of the checkout boy, and snapped his picture. The young man in question didn't pose for the picture. He had no idea that a picture had been taken. Certainly, no modeling release was signed. He was just *there*, doing his job.

Lesson Number One: In the world of Big Data, with mobile, Internet-connected cameras in every pocket, we are always just a few clicks away from being everywhere. The young man whose picture went viral got a real-life taste of that fact when his total lack of privacy became apparent; he became an Internet sensation by doing nothing but bagging products at the checkout counter.

More than 500 million photographs are uploaded to major websites every day. More than 2 billion pictures are taken on mobile devices every day. Factor in webcams and other surveillance devices, and the chances that your image *isn't* somewhere on the Internet are right up there with becoming the next Dalai Lama.

Alex Lee experienced one of these countless daily intrusions that happen in our social media–obsessed society. He won the jackpot in the "privacy is on life support" sweepstakes. It didn't matter that he was tending to his own business. His *existence* created the potential for a transaction—one that required neither his consent nor his participation. The snapping of his picture underscored a simple reality: If you're out in the world, the world can look at you. And if the world has a smartphone, it can snap, store, share, and reshare you, all in just a few taps, each one a little theft of your face, your identity, your self.

In this particular instance, someone grabbed Brooklyn's snapshot from her Twitter account and put it on another social networking site, Tumblr. Brooklyn had no idea. Meanwhile, the picture started replicating on Twitter accounts. While the complexity of the picture's distribution was at least potentially knowable, it was in no way controllable. The million "little thefts" that made Alex Lee famous are metaphorical. No court of law would rule that Brooklyn's actions, or any of the actions of other people who retweeted her photo, rise to the level of theft. But, well, you get the picture—as did millions of people around the world.

Needless to say, Alex Lee had no idea any of this was happening. He hadn't done anything wrong or unusual. There were no regrettable posts, no questionable sites visited, no malware behind it all. His phone wasn't even powered on when the

> **Desirable information goes wherever it's wanted.**

month-long distribution of his image reached critical mass the following Sunday sometime during the Cowboys-Packers game. It was right after that game that Brooklyn first noticed something was afoot on Twitter. She started getting mentioned in posts even though she didn't have very many followers. Her surreptitious shot of Alanna's crush with the waterfall of Justin Bieber hair was getting love from people she didn't know. Among those taking a shine to the checkout boy was a teenager in the UK who had liberated the picture of Alex from a Tumblr user, who had pinched it from Brooklyn's original reply tweet to her friend Alanna. The British girl's tweet was simple: "YOOOOOOOOOO."

A long line formed at Alex Lee's checkout station. It was filled with giggling girls. The reason Alex had turned off his phone was the banal stuff of disorganized people everywhere—no charger, low battery, and needing to get in touch with his parents when his shift was over so they could come pick him up. It was his manager—a senior in high school—who told him what was going on, showing him the picture that had started to go viral. By the time he turned on his phone in the front seat of his mother's Mercedes at the end of his shift, he had more than 100,000 followers, virtually all of whom were new that day. That number would triple before the end of the twenty-four-hour clickstorm set off by the Twitter user named @_twerkcam, who retweeted the "YOOOOOOOOOO" tweet with the hashtag that launched a million mentions—#AlexFromTarget. Brooklyn Reiff's picture had gone viral.

Alex's first tweet was a bit disingenuous. "Am I famous now?" he wrote. That of course got retweeted 42,000 times and was favorited by more than 86,000 users. The hashtag became a trending topic, and talk show host Ellen DeGeneres used it, tweeting, "Hey #AlexFromTarget, it's #EllenFromEllen."

Something else happened, too. According to the *New York Times*, Alex Lee received death threats against him and his family. He had to change his phone number because someone had leaked it—or his phone was hacked. The device failed, unable to keep up with all the texts that came streaming in.

> YOOOOOOOOOO.
> There is no such thing as harmless personal information.

These last details of the #AlexFromTarget story got precisely one buried paragraph in the *Times*. Regardless, though, they highlight the nature of the identity theft problem.

It's important to point out at the outset that it's highly unlikely the Lee family was singularly lax about their personally identifiable information (PII). They didn't do an Edith Byrd, the woman who famously held up her Medicare card during Bill Clinton's speech at the Democratic National Convention in 2012, showing millions of potential identity thieves her name, enrollment date (the next best thing to a date of birth), and Social Security number. The Lee family's information was likely already "out there"— either on the so-called dark web, where dangerous hackers trade other people's secrets for money (or Bitcoins), or on a public-facing database. The reality illustrated in the breach of the Lee family is very simple, and should be a guiding principle in the way you think of your personally identifiable information: The only thing a hacker really needs to get your PII is a little motivation.

The Lee family's personal information was leaked online within hours of the viral explosion of #AlexFromTarget, and the cache of exposed data included some serious digits: bank account numbers, Social Security numbers, and phone records. Worried about the safety of Alex and his five siblings, his parents spent many frenzied hours reaching out to school officials, the police, and security companies.

You Get Around

If you look at Brooklyn Reiff's Twitter account now, it says, among other things, "I want a Jeep to mud in." She is an ordinary Texas teenager. Alanna Page is still posting pictures of cute guys. Alex Lee, however, has ceased being an ordinary teenager. Those humble checkout boy days behind him, he now has more than 700,000 followers on Twitter, and a Gmail account set up for business. Ellen DeGeneres had him on her show, and gave him an iPad so he could tweet more. One would imagine a free Jeep to go mudding in could be his for the asking. A typical tweet informed followers: "Eating pizza and watching Netflix all day. . . . Best day ever." With a national tour scheduled where Alex will do nothing more than appear—he has no special talents—it seems logical to wonder if Netflix paid to be a part of Alex's perfect Sunday.

Alex's story reveals something normally left obscure. It chronicles the way information moves around—in this instance how a tweet about a checkout boy's cuteness turned into photographic evidence of the same, which then got grabbed by random users of social media until it was flicked into the upper climes of the Twittersphere by the fluke of a superuser who just happened to be online at the precise moment when the picture started taking flight—a case of the right tweet in a perfect alignment of tweeps.

Alex Lee's story is also a good example of what we might call "information unicity." The Merriam-Webster dictionary defines unicity as "the quality or state of being unique of its kind." Information unicity is the trail of breadcrumbs we all leave on the Internet. This trail allowed tweeps and journalists alike to figure out that Alex Lee of Frisco, Texas, was #AlexFromTarget. If you know how to look for it, you can find time stamps, locations, and other data that leads all the way back to Alanna Page's tweet, "hello alex check out boy @ target." Many different arrangements of particular kinds of information can point to the same person, place, or thing, and that's how Alex Lee and his family got hacked.

Alex from Target, of course, is an actual young man, but mostly he's just #AlexFromTarget, an idea more than a person, something people talk about on social media. He could be a person or a marketing promotion or something in between—but it hardly matters. To data sleuths and cyberslime alike, he's just another potential source of value, another identity to mine for profit. And he's a lot easier to dig up than buried gold.

The first thing to try is finding the source of the meme and working outward. Let's say the photo of Alex Lee wasn't geotagged, no other identifying information was embedded in the photograph, and location services were turned off on both girls' Twitter accounts. None of that stuff is necessary. We already know Alex works at Target; it's pinned to his shirt. Going back to the originating tweet, we see that Alanna Page is from the Dallas area, and Brooklyn Reiff is from Prosper. Using those two data points alone—where Alanna and Brooklyn live—anyone who wanted to find Alex could have done so easily by entering Prosper into Target's online store-locator tool. The closest Target: Frisco.

Unless you live on a primitive, deserted island, you almost certainly have identifying data, your digital fingerprints. This data, your information unicity, is what distinguishes you from anyone else. It's how a line of teenage girls located Alex Lee's checkout counter, and how the death threats found their way to Alex's home. It's also how the Lee family's Social Security numbers got leaked along with Alex's mobile phone number. Numbers, dates, schools attended, clubs, hobbies, race results, family and friends—they all can be used to pin a name to the disparate facts that comprise us on paper. Our personally identifiable information is everywhere, and of course there are people who make money deploying the information unicity of complete strangers. They are good at

---

Social Media Can Get You Got

Facebook and other social media sites can be an identity thief's El Dorado (not to be confused with Eldorado Parkway in Frisco, Texas, where Alex Lee worked at Target).

The more you share about your life, the more opportunities an identity thief has to piece together what might be your response to security questions and zero in on zeroing out your financial resources.

---

cobbling together different clusters of information that point at you, and only you, and then using that information to get more information, until they can convince someone in a position to hand over goods or services (or someone who approves credit applications) that they are you, and "you" want whatever it is your identity thief desires.

In this new information landscape, everyone is a celebrity. It doesn't matter who you are, and the only reason everyone hasn't become a victim of identity-related crime is the backlog. If you are in any way plugged into the commerce of daily life, your information is out there, and no matter how scrambled and scattered it is, there is someone out there who can make enough sense of it to obtain goods and services (or credit) in your name.

You may be surprised to learn that some of your personal information is publicly available, including possibly detailed lists of items or services you've purchased with a credit or debit card.

Large-scale studies depend on huge data sets comprised of the behavior of thousands of consumers that is collected when we use our smartphones, credit cards, Internet browsers, and many other conveniences of modern life. That information can be utilized for a variety of purposes ranging from assessing traffic patterns to decrease congestion during rush hour to predicting and controlling outbreaks of infectious diseases. These metadata sets are always anonymized. That means you are not you. Names, account numbers, and IP addresses—all the simple stuff that identifies you—are stripped away because they aren't necessary for most of the determinations made by crunching the numbers. It's all about seeing trends and patterns. Companies like Amazon and Facebook use the same kinds of data to serve you content that is most likely to interest you. The main point is that the use of your information is for good, not evil.

Except when it isn't.

The problem is that information can be misused. Sometimes you don't know anything's wrong until you're making a purchase at a checkout counter and your credit card is declined, or you get a phone call at your home in Nantucket ("Can you confirm a purchase of $502.35 at BJ's Wholesale Club in Honolulu?"), or you are buying a car or trying to refinance your house and learn that your credit score is too low—shot to hell by a process that didn't happen on Twitter or Facebook, but that may have been aided by the things you shared there.

> Trust but verify: Anonymized data is publicly available because it's thought to be safe, but it may not be as anonymous as you think.

Your undoing happened in less public forums, many of them tucked away on so-called deep web sites or on the dark web (about which more later). It was your Social Security number, or some combination of seemingly harmless information like your email address, your mother's maiden name, and your birthday, that gave a criminal just enough information about you so that he or she could poke around social media and glean the kinds of information that show up in security questions, like where you've lived, what companies you've worked for, the names of pets past and present, and schools attended or their mascots.

Alex from Target's story is a parable about the ways in which we're all exposed. It's about the myriad ways we are vulnerable—

financially or personally—and how woefully unprotected we are against various kinds of intrusion.

As the reach of social media extends to ever more remote segments of the market, anyone who cares to take a look can with relative ease become acquainted with the particular aspects of your life that banks and other financial institutions use to determine your unicity— that you are who you claim to be—before green-lighting a transaction. While the process of how something goes viral is fundamentally unknowable, a forensic approach can reveal how a particular viral message or meme traveled from point of origin to tipping point. Unfortunately, that forensics approach only works after the fact in a postmortem examination.

> **We Are All Already Exposed**
>
> The pieces of your information puzzle are out there waiting for the wrong person with the right skills to piece together your digital "you" and use it to defraud you.

As Brooklyn said in an interview with Yahoo shortly after #AlexFromTarget entered the popular lexicon, "This shows you how fast something can go viral. It's, like, scary. It really is. Because if you say one wrong thing your life could be over, basically."

If the wrong person gets his or her grubby little fingers on your private information, Brooklyn is absolutely right, "Your life could be over, basically." If that seems like hyperbole, put it this way: Your life as you now know it could well be over. Alex Lee's parents know this firsthand, even as their son goes on to reap the random fortune that the Twittersphere laid at his feet.

The chances that you are reading this book right now just for fun and have not yet become a victim of some form of identity-related crime are declining by the minute. Worse yet are the chances that at least some of your personally identifiable information hasn't already been either used to commit a crime (this would include one of those phishing emails that regularly wind up in your inbox or trash folder) or bundled with other kinds of information to be sold in a criminal transaction. Major data breaches are now commonplace.

Credit card numbers get stolen all the time. You get those phone calls informing you that a new card is in the mail, and it's no longer even alarming. It's just the way things are. But credit card fraud is sometimes just the beginning. In the right (or wrong) hands, the Lee family's Social Security numbers were worth a pretty penny, and really could have forever changed the fate of that family. That discrete arrangement of nine digits is to personal information what DNA is to your body. Using nothing but bank account information and these essential digits, a tremendous amount of damage can be done.

The "virus" of identity theft relies on cracking your information unicity. It needs you to be you when it drills down into the personal information "DNA" that comprises who you are financially, because everything it can grab requires an accurate impersonation of your digital persona. Unicity is necessary to this kind of fraud. Ironically, the instant stardom Alex Lee experienced was probably the only reason serious damage wasn't inflicted on him and his family. They were under siege because of the #AlexFrom-Target hashtag, which placed them on high alert, so they found out quickly when they were compromised.

For most of us, the most essential fact of our digital lives is embedded in the Alex Lee story: You're going to get got. But instead of a sip at the fountain of fame and a chance to monetize a no-longer-trending hashtag on Twitter, you may be ruined. The point is that our level of exposure is the same as Alex's when he was an anonymous teenager working at Target in Frisco, Texas. Our most sensitive personally identifiable information is already in the wrong hands—so we need to be as vigilant as if we were overnight celebrities. We can't wait to become the victims of serious, and sometimes prolonged, fraud.

You are your Social Security number. Consider for a moment all the places that have those nine digits, from memberships dating back to your childhood, to old jobs at places that probably stored your personnel file in a storage facility—or sent it

> Your Social Security number is the skeleton key to your finances past, present, and future.

to a landfill—to doctors, health insurers, and accountants. Then consider the major breaches of recent years—and the not so major breaches at smaller organizations that never made the nightly news. There is no way to know whether your Social Security number has been sold, stolen, or both. But it probably has.

There are as many ways for your personal information to wind up in enemy territory as there are databases and filing cabinets that store your personal information. Data breaches are an increasingly common way for your information to get out there. The 2013 Target breach exposed the financial and personal information of perhaps as many as 100 million people. Then came the aftershocks—reports in January 2014 of similar hits at Sally's Beauty and Neiman Marcus. There was another big breach at White Lodging, the giant hotel and restaurant management chain. There were still more breaches at Home Depot, Adobe, JPMorgan Chase, eBay, and others. Then came the Sony hack, which not only exposed the personally identifiable information of tens of thousands of Sony employees and stars, but actually forced the company to initially cancel the theatrical release of what was supposed to be their big Christmas movie, *The Interview*, after major theaters decided it was too risky to show the film. The hits keep coming. In January 2015, headlines screamed that some 80 million customers of Anthem were exposed in a giant breach. In March 2015, Premera began notifying 11 million members that personal information (including Social Security numbers and medical records) had been exposed by persons unknown. In June 2015, the Office of Personnel Management, in effect, the human resources department of the United States, announced perhaps the most devastating breaches of all with anywhere between 18 and 32 million (possibly higher) records involved—including millions of background checks for present and former government employees, contractors, family members of candidates, and even their friends. Numbers don't lie. Since 2005, more than a billion sensitive records with personally identifiable information have been leaked. That information is not unified. It is not organized. It is most likely in the hands of several different criminal enterprises that have bought and sold it multiple times. Regardless, it is out there, and there are people who make a seriously good living working on the puzzle of personally identifiable information that is available, piecing it together into useable blocks of reidentified information that can be used in the commission of fraud.

An example of the myriad ways data can be used by criminals comes from a report in *Science Magazine*, which revealed the soft underbelly of what was once considered a well-armored use of "anonymized" consumer information. As it turns out, it's not so well armored after all. In fact, anonymized data may offer no more protection than you'd get by leaving your Social Security card in plain view in a good neighborhood. All that seems to matter is whether someone with bad intentions gets hold of it.

The study's authors were able to successfully identify consumers based on several anonymized data sets. Using publicly available metadata with no credit card numbers, names, or any other identifiers, the report's coauthors were able to connect a specific person to specific purchases using just three factors: a receipt, an Instagram post, and a Tweet about a new purchase or a Facebook post that included the location of a favorite bar or a restaurant frequently visited. And in case you're wondering if this was some kind of fluke or exceptional case, lead author Yves-Alexandre de Montjoye was successful more than 90 percent of the time.

The discovery that two or three purchases in a metadata set containing millions of transactions can be pegged to a specific person raises a rather obvious question as to whether data sets that track large-scale human behavior should be made available to the public.

Anonymized data helps scientists figure things out. It's the social information equivalent of being an organ donor, only less severe and completely involuntary. Because it involves only random pieces of your story that have been excised from anything that might be linked to you, it's supposed to be okay. But at least when you donate an organ, you're helping another person. The "doctors" who harvest your data don't have MDs, and they aren't necessarily going to use your specific information to fix anything. Many of them just want your information so they can better understand how to make money from you.

It's easier than it looks to find the people behind anonymized data—including you.

Details about purchases, phone calls made, places visited—stripped of the identifiers (such as account numbers, IP addresses, email accounts, names, addresses, and credit card numbers) that connect them to specific people—are regularly used by the government, private researchers, and consumer-facing enterprises. These so-called metadata sets contain detailed information regarding the media large groups of people regularly consume, where we've been, what we did when we were there, what food we like, what sorts of illnesses we've contracted as a result, and how we got better (or didn't). In theory, these huge samples of human behavior could hold the key to addressing many kinds of problems—everything from the way we fight diseases and feed the world's population to how we find the best deal on a new car or the fastest commute from Point A to Point B. Metadata is also used to *stop* identity thieves from using purloined credit card information—specifically by monitoring purchases and sounding the alarm when something doesn't match the purchasing history for a particular credit card holder.

And all this is OK because the use of your information—scrubbed and swept and disconnected from your personal identity—is being used for good, not evil. At least, that's how it works in theory.

This is one reason that it would be a mistake to stop collecting anonymized data, or even to stop publishing it. As the author of the study, Yves-Alexandre de Montjoye, explains, "The transformational potential of metadata data sets is . . . conditional on their wide availability." Scientists need whatever data they are using to be available to their peers so that their work can be checked and verified, challenged and improved. Progress requires it. According to the report, "Several publishers and funding agencies now require experimental data to be publicly available." So, increasingly, data of all kinds is available publicly. Just as it should be.

The real problem is not that this data is public—it's that it's not truly anonymous. That's what de Montjoye's study really proved.

Social Media Posts That Can Get You Got

- Real-time pictures from vacation (you're begging burglars to rob you)
- Announcements of upcoming trips
- Photos of your home, car, and valuables
- Class reunion, school attended, degrees, dates
- Birthdays and other important anniversaries
- Your phone number or email address
- Photos of new passports, driver's licenses, your first credit or debit card, and other identifying documents
- New purchases
- Meals and other social outings
- Pets and kids (their names are often used in security questions)

Here's something else it showed: Social media can make your identity much easier to crack. Remember that de Montjoye used posts from Instagram, Facebook, and Twitter to triangulate the identities of people in his sample metadata sets. But the problem doesn't end there. Whatever you put out there can be seen by people who may have a particular crime in mind for you based on what you post.

Does the *Science* study mean that the government should shut down the public's access to metadata sets? I don't think so. There is too much to gain from that information remaining publicly available. Does it mean everyone should stop using social media? Again, not so far as I can tell. The new data landscape brings great rewards, but also new risks. Organizations can do their part by finding ways to make metadata sets harder to decode. You can help yourself by not using social media to broadcast your purchases, your location, or other identifying facts. Or, if that's too much of a sacrifice, here's another option: You can still post that stuff, but think like a thief, and then make your posts (or at least some of them) inaccurate. Cover your tracks not by sweeping them away, but by making too many to follow.

This is a sound strategy, but remember it's not a solution. There is no solution; there are only best practices and knowledge. Even if you do everything right, you need to assume that your information has been (or will be) used against you. Your job is to be like Alex Lee's family: on high alert. That way, you can detect the scam before it causes real damage.

It doesn't matter who you are. It doesn't matter how many transaction alerts are set up. The only reason everyone hasn't become a victim of identity-related crime is that the bad guys just haven't gotten around to them yet.

Think of this as a bandwidth issue: There simply aren't enough identity thieves to harvest all the lost and free-floating information that's out there. It pays to be paranoid here. Assume that the bad guys figured out de Montjoye's method of reidentification long ago—or something that works just as well.

The bottom line: If you are in any way plugged into the commerce of daily life, your information is out there, and it is only a matter of time before you become a victim of an identity-related crime. But while this seems like a problem (and it sure is), it's not the end of the world. It's a situation that can be handled.

2

A Short History of Identity (and Fraud)

(And You Thought It Was Just About Credit Cards)

MORTICIAN: Who's that then?
CUSTOMER: I don't know.
MORTICIAN: Must be a king.
CUSTOMER: Why?
MORTICIAN: He hasn't got shit all over him.

—*MONTY PYTHON AND THE HOLY GRAIL*

On a gloriously crisp day in February 1910, the prince of Abyssinia and his entourage were welcomed with fanfare aboard the mighty British battleship *Dreadnought*. The captain and his entire crew turned out in dress whites in honor of their guests. During this visit the prince and his retinue were treated with all the respect due to people of their standing, and the captain personally conducted a tour of the great warship. Reports of the day indicate they departed to an especially stirring rendition of "God Save the King."

It was revealed the following day to be an elaborate hoax. The prince of Abyssinia wasn't a prince at all—he was one among a group of young upper-crust pranksters wearing blackface. (Another of them was a young woman named Adeline Virginia Stephen, who would later be known as the rising literary talent Virginia Woolf.)

19

Reliable mechanisms for verifying a person's identity are a relatively recent development. But the quest for such systems is much longer, and it makes for a fascinating story—and the evolution of identity over some 10,000 years is only the first part of it. We must not allow today's pandemic of identity theft to be the punch line.

Identity theft is as old as the Bible. In Genesis, Jacob covered himself with goatskins and impersonated his brother, Esau, to trick their father into giving him the blessing of the firstborn, which bestowed upon him all the family property—and, some say, resulted in the strife that has plagued the Middle East for thousands of years.

A thousand years ago, a person could become almost anyone they wanted to be simply by claiming to be that person. Today, armed with enough personally identifiable information (birth dates, maiden names, previous addresses, phone numbers, credit profiles, and Social Security numbers), a person can go online and become almost anyone they want, simply by typing in the right information.

And your name is . . . ?
And you do what?

While you are unique, your name isn't. In many cases, individuals may share their name with hundreds or even thousands of other people. Your name is little more than a label that has been affixed to your life, and that name alone is not sufficient to prove you are who you claim to be. However, for thousands of years, a name was the only means we had to identify a specific person.

The quest for individual identity began when Adam and Eve began their begetting. Anthropologists believe that members of the most primitive societies were first identified by the specific sounds they made. A mimicked version of those sounds became the way they were known; it became their name.

"Hey, there's E-Ee-E-EeEEEee over there!"

Surprisingly, while we take it for granted that everyone in the world has a name, there is no universally accepted standard for the common usage of those names.

Thousands of years ago, when people tended to stay in the general area where they were born, and lived among a small group of people, a first name was sufficient ("You can call me Paul!"). But as populations grew, and two or more people had the same first name, additional identifiers were needed, so people became known by their occupation or where they lived, an accomplishment in battle or who their father was. During his lifetime, Jesus Christ was known as Jesus of Nazareth, or Jesus, son of Joseph. Only after his death did he become known as Jesus Christ, with "Christ" being the translation of the Hebrew word meaning "Messiah." So, he was then referred to as Jesus, Christ the Messiah, rather than the name we know him by today. While there were many Leonardos, the one we remember and honor is Leonardo of the town of Vinci—Leonardo da Vinci.

Eventually, second names—surnames—became the accepted means of identifying people. Different cultures had different rules for surnames. In Europe, a person went by their first, middle, and last—or family—name. In China, the family name comes first and the given name comes last. In many Spanish-speaking countries, the family name is in the middle position. Sikh men and most Sikh women share the same last name, making identification by name difficult. In some societies, when women marry it is customary that they take their husband's family name; in other cultures they do not.

Last names finally became an accepted part of standard usage in Western cultures during the 1600s. By that time, cities had grown larger, churches began recording marriages and baptisms, armies started to keep detailed records, and nonroyals became participants in the economic system, so it finally became necessary for institutions to be able to identify specific individuals.

Yet accomplishing this was easier said than done. Most people didn't have identity documents—why would they?—and photography hadn't been invented. The only possible means of positively identifying a specific individual was through eyewitness identification. Someone else who knew that person was required to confirm their identity, and that simply didn't happen very often. So a person could easily assume the identity of whomever he or she wanted to be.

After the Roman emperor Nero committed suicide, several men alleged that his death had been faked, and each claimed to be the former emperor. One enterprising imposter even formed a small militia and became a pirate. Eventually he was caught and beheaded.

Following Joan of Arc's execution, a number of people alleged that at the last second another woman had been substituted for Joan of Orléans and burned at the stake in her place. One of these imposters was positively identified as Joan by her brothers and continued her charade for almost five years, being welcomed by nobles and receiving expensive gifts during that time.

Continuing for several thousand years into modern Western civilization, there was no way of definitively identifying an individual. That stretch of time is replete with fascinating tales of imposters.

George Psalmanazar became quite famous throughout Northern Europe in 1700 as the first native of Taiwan—then known as Formosa—to visit Europe. He spun chilling yarns about life in his distant homeland, claiming that Formosans were polygamous and permitted by law to eat their wives as punishment for infidelity. After six years, and the publication of his book, *An Historical and Geographical Description of Formosa*, he revealed that it had been a hoax.

Perhaps the best-known imposter is the Frenchman Martin Guerre. In 1538, Guerre disappeared, and eight years later a man showed up claiming to be him. Guerre's wife accepted him as her husband and lived with him for three years, bearing two children. When Guerre sued an uncle for his family inheritance, he was accused of being a fraud. The case went through several trials and appeals. It appeared he would be vindicated, but then the real Martin Guerre returned, having lost a leg while serving in the Spanish army. The imposter was executed.

While modern imposters are required to produce an array of facts and documents to support their false identities, that hasn't stopped them. Among the most successful were the "Great Imposter," Ferdinand Demara, who stole a range of identities from that of a Trappist monk to that of a Canadian Navy surgeon, and Frank Abagnale Jr., who conned his way to millions of dollars by posing as a Pan Am pilot, a doctor, and a prosecutor, as told in the book and movie, *Catch Me If You Can.*

The first steps toward being able to positively identify an individual began early in the 1800s with the establishment of municipal police forces, which needed to identify suspects and criminals. Centuries earlier, the Romans and Greeks would tattoo or brand prisoners, while the Chinese would cut off a finger or a limb. ("That'll be one tattoo, please.") Tattoos were very useful for identification. The Maori of New Zealand had symbols tattooed on their faces. Each person's symbols—called "mokos"—were unique, and the same symbol was used to identify the owner of land or even drawn as a signature whenever a written contract was required. Perhaps not surprisingly, written signatures have never been especially valued for identification. As far back as the era of Socrates, criminals have been forging documents.

While individuals had little need to be identified, with the exception of proving identity in inheritance cases, increasingly urbanized societies had a growing need to accurately identify specific individuals. Various methods employed by the police gradually became adopted throughout society. One of the initial methods employed by law enforcement, as recounted in *Les Misérables*, was to have people with photographic memories visit prisons regularly to look at all the new arrivals to see if there was a repeat offender they recognized and to commit the faces of the new prisoners to memory.

Actual photography was first used in Belgian prisons in the 1840s—the birth of the mug shot. However, the quality of pictures was so poor at that time, prisoners needed only to make faces—mug at the camera—to foil that form of identification. There was also no practical way to reproduce these pictures. As it was virtually impossible to check every previously existing photo, there was little value in using photographs for identification. Criminals simply would provide false names as well as employ various methods to alter their physical appearance in order to beat the rap. Criminal identification clearly had a ways to go.

The first widely accepted means of proving the identity of a known criminal was invented by the Frenchman Alphonse Bertillon in 1879. The Bertillon system, as it became known universally, was a compilation of eleven different body measurements, including the spread of an individual's arms, the length of the left foot, and the circumference of the skull above the eyes. It also noted body markings, including tattoos. While this system certainly wasn't precise, the odds of two people having the same Bertillon measurements were said to be about 300 million to one. For more than two decades, the Bertillon system remained the accepted means of identification throughout Europe and the United States, and might have stayed that way if a man named Will West hadn't been convicted of murder and sent to Leavenworth prison in 1903.

According to legend, when West's Bertillon measurements were taken, officials discovered that there was another inmate at the same prison, also named Will West, who was serving a life sentence for murder. The two men had almost exactly the same measurements. As it turned out, Will West One and Two—who were unknown to each other—were identical twin brothers. The only difference between the two men was their fingerprints. The next day, Leavenworth Prison officials began to rely on fingerprints as the primary means of proving identification, and within months most other American prisons followed suit.

Fingerprints have been used in various places and at different times throughout history as a means of determining a person's identity. In third-century China, merchants used fingerprints in wax to seal business contracts. In fourteenth-century Persia, government documents required a fingerprint seal. As early as 1686, a professor of anatomy at Italy's University of Bologna, Marcello Malpighi, noted and named the characteristics common to all fingerprints, including ridges, whorls, and spirals. In 1858, British chief magistrate Sir William Herschel, working in India, began insisting that Indians seal contracts with a fingerprint in addition to a signature as a means of ensuring they would not attempt to repudiate the agreement. It took some time to gain universal acceptance, but eventually the Herschels of the world came to believe that no two prints were exactly alike, and it was possible to identify an individual simply by comparing his fingerprint to a known sample. So, fingerprints became the accepted means of proving identity.

It was almost twenty-five years later, in 1882, that an employee of the U.S. Geological Survey working in New Mexico stamped his own fingerprint on a document to guard against forgery. It was the first documented time a fingerprint had been used to prove identity in the New World. A year later, Mark Twain's *Life on the Mississippi* told the story of a murderer who is identified by the use of fingerprints.

In 1892, Argentinean police officer Juan Vucetich successfully matched a bloody fingerprint found on the doorpost at a murder scene to the mother of the two victims. It was the first attempt to use fingerprints to identify a killer, and it proved to be accurate: The woman confessed. Exactly a decade later, the famed Alphonse Bertillon, who by this time had become the director of the Paris

Police Department's Bureau of Identification, successfully matched a fingerprint found at a crime scene to prints on file—the first time a fingerprint had been used to solve a crime in which there was no suspect. Doubtless the irony was not lost on Bertillon, whose own detective work contributed to the demise of the eponymous system of identification that made him famous.

Faking or hiding fingerprints is much more difficult than forging signatures or making faces at a camera. Many people have tried, but, almost without exception, they failed. Some of the more interesting fugitives of fingerprint justice include John Dillinger, who in 1934 dipped his fingers in acid in a failed attempt to destroy his fingerprints, and Colombian drug lord Daniel "El Loco" Barrera, who tried the same method—with the same failed results—in 2012. Another criminal sliced off his fingertips, then literally had his fingers sewn to his chest—where the skin has no ridges—until they healed, leaving him without fingerprints. He was caught: His recorded prints included an impression of the lines and swirls below the first joint, which were used to match the prints and prove his identity. Another felon in hiding cut the skin off his fingertips, sliced it into smaller pieces, and then put those pieces back on his fingers in a different arrangement, creating entirely new and bizarre prints. He was also caught: An FBI fingerprint expert cut up photographs of the new prints, then painstakingly reassembled them as if solving a gigantic jigsaw puzzle.

At the beginning of the twentieth century, with the invention of the automobile and the airplane, the positive identification of an individual became a more pressing issue. For the first time, it was possible for ordinary people to travel routinely beyond their towns to places where they weren't known by neighbors or local merchants, where they had to prove their identity to strangers. And, as there had never been a need to do that, there was no way of doing it. Con men similar to *The Music Man*'s fictional Harold Hill moved easily from town to town, making outrageous claims and selling their fraudulent products, then slipping out of town on the midnight express before the latest scam could be uncovered.

The use of documents as a means of identification became relatively common in the early 1900s. While birth certificates had been issued throughout history almost exclusively to the children of nobles to maintain aristocratic lineage and ensure inheritances, most other births were simply registered at the parish church or, when necessary, city hall. In many parts of the United States, birth certificates, which most people assume have always served as an important legal record, were not regularly issued until World War II.

All the information or documents that we use to confirm our identity these days—Social Security numbers, driver's licenses, birth certificates, even passports—are modern creations.

The driver's license, probably the most commonly accepted form of identification, originally had absolutely nothing to do with an individual's ability to drive, and in most states wasn't even mandatory. The initial purpose of a driver's license was to raise tax dollars. Only people driving for commercial purposes—cab and truck drivers—were required to obtain licenses, because the government had the right to tax and regulate commerce. It didn't extend to noncommercial uses. In fact, when the state of Illinois attempted to force drivers to obtain and carry licenses, the Illinois Supreme Court ruled that it was an "unjustifiable, unconscionable and unconstitutional intrusion on the rights of individuals to travel upon the public highways unhindered and unimpaired."

It wasn't until the middle of the twentieth century that most states began requiring individuals to get a driver's license, which was about the time that licenses began to be used and accepted as a manifestation of identification. States then began requiring more information on a license, and some states didn't add photographs until the 1980s.

Ironically, the Illinois decision was never repealed or over-turned, which means that the Illinois state law prohibiting people from driving without a license might just be unconstitutional.

Passports have a long and appropriately murky history, dating back to the Old Testament when King Artaxerxes of Persia gave an adviser a letter addressed "to the governors beyond the river," requesting the adviser's safe passage across their lands. While no one knows for certain, the word "passport" is believed to have referred to passage through the gates of a city entrance—the "porte"—although many assume it had something to do with seaports. England's Henry V is given credit for the creation of the modern passport in 1414—a document that served as a record of places visited as well as an identification document. In 1858, Britain recognized the passport as an identification document, although it was still not required for international travel.

Prior to World War I, few European nations required a pass-port to enter or leave the country, but at the beginning of the war, countries began enforcing passport regulations as a means of detecting spies. It was during this period that photographs were first attached to passports.

Later, as World War II spread through Europe, passports took on an entirely new meaning. The words, "Your documents please," became a chilling reminder of how vulnerable an individual could be if he or she had the wrong identity. Papers that proved an "acceptable" identity became extremely valuable during the Nazis' Final Solution. In numerous cases, possession of a forged passport literally meant the difference between life and death, and the creation of documents that would pass inspection be-came an art.

The use of documents to authenticate identity isn't foolproof, because they can be forged. With an officially stamped photo-graph, a passport can be faked, which is why fingerprints became so important for making a positive identification.

The first Social Security number was issued in November 1936. A precursor to the American Express mantra, people tended to never leave home without their Social Security card. For a while, some people even had their number tattooed on their body in plain sight. Few bothered to take precautions to protect their SSN. While important to each individual, it had little value to anyone else. In fact, several decades passed before banks began using it for identification purposes. Eventually, however, the Social Security number became associated with checking accounts, credit cards, and mortgages—indeed, all forms of credit transactions. And with that transition, the Social Security number became enormously more important.

Knowing a Social Security number and the name associated with it opened the door to a treasure trove of personal information that could be used for various illegal purposes. For criminals, a Social Security number became the gift that kept on giving, and, for victims, the curse that kept on taking. Once they had your number and enough information about you to answer a few questions—where you were born, your mother's maiden name, and so on—they could and did do whatever they wanted in your name.

Before e-commerce and social networking made identity theft a big player in twenty-first-century crime, the most common form of identity caper was when underage students used fake identification to get served in bars. That began to change in the mid-1970s, when, according to Secret Service lore, a group of Nigerian students with expiring visas were determined to find a way to remain in the United States. By buying, stealing, forging, or simply finding documentation, they were able to create new identities that enabled them to successfully evade the authorities. Once the ability to create new identities spread, it was only a matter of time before people started using them to commit financial crimes or worse.

An individual's identity no longer had a direct connection to what a person looked like, or whether their fingerprints matched a sample, or whether they were even a person—human beings distinguished by numbers and facts on file had no flesh and blood, and they could be in the next room, or on the other side of the world, and no one would ever know. They were collections of information—their existence was a composite of stolen numbers and discrete facts. Individual identity was unguarded everywhere, ripe for the picking, and as a result every piece of personal and financial information that became available to those smart enough to figure out how to exploit it began to find their way into the identity thief's tool kit.

In 1983, the discovery of the polymerase chain reaction suddenly made DNA profiling available and affordable. DNA made it possible, for the first time in history, to identify a specific individual almost to the exclusion of every other person in the world.

In the early 1980s, law enforcement personnel in England were able to extract a DNA sample from the body of a murder victim, but found no obvious suspects to try to match it to. British police asked the male residents of the town in which the victim was found to voluntarily offer a DNA sample. Those samples were tested for their DNA signature, but no match was found. Then someone informed the authorities that a friend admitted to providing urine instead. When this friend's actual DNA was tested, it matched the DNA found on the victim's body. With that, DNA became the accepted means of proving an individual's identity. Even in complex inheritance cases, in which fingerprints play no role, a familial relationship could be proven or disproven. After thousands of years, it had finally become possible for an individual to prove his or her identity beyond the shadow of a doubt.

The centuries-long saga in which identity was something one could fake or forage off a gravestone, totally impervious to challenge, had come to an end. This conclusive method for positively identifying individuals tracked closely with a startling new application of a totally different kind of technology, one that fundamentally changed the way we live and the meaning of identity: computers.

Until the dawn of the digital age, an individual's identity actually had little value, so little, in fact, that few people bothered to take the precautions necessary to protect the sensitive personal information required to prove they were who they claimed to be. Frankly, it was too much trouble for too little purpose. Worst case, someone would lose a credit card, or have it stolen, and the thief would charge up a storm. It was a nuisance that might end up costing the victim a few bucks, but it wasn't a life-changing event. Even if someone did manage to steal the identity of another, there wasn't a whole lot they could do with it anyway.

As is generally the way on the march of progress, the moment social systems and commerce created the means for an individual to authenticate his or her unique identity, criminals discovered ways to exploit those same systems to make that identity extraordinarily valuable. The rise of digital everything was a great boon. Slowly at first, but then in a great wave of acceptance, people began putting their entire lives into cyberspace. They did their banking and paid bills, shopped with credit cards, joined community forums, met people, posted photographs, shared their innermost secrets, and freely identified many of their contacts on multiple public websites. In so doing, they unwittingly created a complete online persona—a cyber version of themselves.

The digital footprint emerged as a concept, and then as a means of identification. In response, a new type of crime—identity theft—took flight, and it morphed into something well beyond the use of stolen identification to compromise a credit account. Once an identity thief captured an individual's Social Security number and compiled a sufficient amount of personally identifiable information to convincingly impersonate the victim, there was almost nothing he or she couldn't or wouldn't do.

3

Swiping Happens

When it comes to identity theft, people have many questions and few answers. Should I shred sensitive documents? (Yes.) Is it worse to lose a wallet, a smartphone, or a computer? (It depends on how much sensitive information they contain.) Does it really matter if all of the logins and passwords for my online accounts are the same? (Yes, it really does.) How common is identity theft? (Very.) What are my chances of being defrauded by identity thieves? (The odds are ever in their favor.) Is there anything I can do to avoid becoming a victim? (No.)

Identity theft is the worst kind of dumb luck. You can do a number of things to keep it from ruining your life, but there isn't much you can do to stop it from happening to you. Identity thieves are like coyotes: They wander around looking for scraps. They take whatever they can find. They are opportunists.

The proposition that you will be able to fence off your property and maintain a completely buttoned-up, coyote-free life while remaining on high alert 24/7 is a pipedream. When the coyotes of Scamville pad your way, there's not much you can do about it. You can hope they don't find a way into your personal finances, or that

---

Cybercrime: You Can't Leave Home Without It

Skimmers are devices that read the magnetic stripe on the back of a credit or debit card when you swipe it to make a purchase or to access your account through an ATM. They record the following data:

- Cardholder's name
- Account number
- Expiration date
- Card security code or verification value

Carefully placed cameras record PIN numbers. With this information, a scammer has everything needed to have an all-expenses-paid shopping trip on your dime, or, worse, to empty out your bank accounts.

Tip: Debit cards increase your exposure to fraud. Use a credit card. They offer better consumer protections, and often have better reward programs.

---

your information camouflage is fail-safe, but no one is that good or that lucky all the time.

As Hunter S. Thompson wrote in *Fear and Loathing in America*, "Luck is a very thin wire between survival and disaster, and not many people can keep their balance on it." If the present book persuades you of nothing else, let it convince you that everyone gets got. If you believe this, or you've already been the victim of an identity-related crime, my hope is that you'll find what you are looking for here.

With very few outlier exceptions, we've all been swiped, scanned, digitized, filed, and disseminated to such a staggering extent that it's impossible to know where our information is and who's had access to it. Unless you live in a log cabin on Loon Lake and do all your business in cash or kind, you're gettable. If you've ever seen a doctor, or if you've ever registered for classes at an institution of higher learning, you're already in the crosshairs of countless identity snipers. If you've ever provided personal information via email, you may be in jeopardy. If you've ever swiped a credit card through a card reader, your chances of being given the gift that keeps on taking are only getting better. If you gave your ZIP code, email address, or telephone number at the cash register of any store you've ever shopped in, you're a target. Every time you roll out of bed, you're entering the identity theft lottery.

This book is for realists. It is not for people who remember every single retailer, medical provider, financial institution, or government agency that has ever collected, stored, and disseminated their personally identifiable information. If you're anything like me, you have no idea where your data is, how (or even if) it's being warehoused, or how long it will be there, wherever "there" happens to be. And, like me, you're already a target. That's the point. We all are.

When it comes to identity theft, cyberattacks, and successful hacks, the difference between us and the rest of the world is not terribly big, but it's nonetheless a crucial one: We use common sense. We don't think we are invincible, and we're pretty sure that it's only a matter of time before we get entangled in a cyberattack. In fact, we assume something is going to go terribly wrong, and we've made it our habit to look for it. The fact that we've swiped our credit cards, debit cards, identity cards, and work badges means we're vulnerable to having our personal information swiped and used

> **Identity Theft Is a Growth Industry**
>
> According to Javelin Strategy and Research, the odds of getting scammed after a data breach in 2010 were one in nine. In 2014, Javelin found that the odds had increased to **one in three**.

Are You Sure No One's Listening?

Before the Internet of Things (IoT), the bad guys had to break into your house and hide a very expensive bug in order to spy on you. (Actually, the device was pretty cheap, but the cost of hiring the guys to do the bugging was noteworthy.) Today, there's a Facebook app and other smartphone features that can do it all at the flick of a fingertip. Perhaps you get a more robust user experience, but at what cost?

---

for all kinds of things. There is one thing that separates us from those who hope that they'll somehow slip the noose of identity theft because, for some magical reason, it will never happen to them: We approach our personal information and the threat of identity theft in a spirit of preparedness. We are as ready as anyone can be for the worst that can (and most likely will) come our way.

The other day, a reporter asked me who's to blame for the growing epidemic of identity-related tax fraud. I could have answered, "the bad guys"—the identity thieves who devote their days to hacking people's accounts and putting their personal information to profitable use. Or I could have said it was the government, which is so overwhelmed by the information security problem that it can't even keep the NSA safe from breaches, never mind the rest of us. But I chose a third answer.

"We're all to blame," I said. And I truly believe it. When it comes to any identity-related crime, the buck stops with you and me, because we're the only ones who can know what's what in time to stop from getting hurt, or at least to move quickly enough to contain the damage.

Breaches, and the identity theft that flows from them, have become the third certainty in life, right behind death and taxes. Your introduction to the fact that you got "got" can take many forms. It may be a call from a debt collector, or the flashing lights of a police car as you are pulled over for missing a stop sign, only to find yourself handcuffed and cooling your heels in jail because someone stole your identity and used it in the commission of a crime. Whatever it is, you're far better off if you can see it coming.

This is one reason the face-saving tactics of hacked companies can be dangerous. Consider the case of Anthem, the second largest healthcare insurer in the United States. Hackers broke into their system in 2014, and accessed unencrypted databases containing the sensitive personal information of some 80 million current and former policyholders and employees. When that happened, tens of millions of people were automatically flung into harm's way.

Oh Baby, Oh Baby

Baby monitors have been hacked and turned into infant-heckling devices, with new parents running into their baby's room to find a stranger yelling obscenities because no one reset a default password setting.

The popular theory of that attack was that the Chinese government was behind it, and they weren't looking for personally identifiable information, but rather trade secrets. The theory was that China wanted to set up a similar health insurance program for its citizens, and hacking Anthem was both cheaper and faster than hiring top health insurance executives to create a plan from scratch.

Now, before you breathe that sigh of relief, reflect upon the fact that this doesn't mean your information is safe. Frankly, the less the Chinese government thinks of its value, the worse it is for you, because they have absolutely no incentive to protect it and quite a bit to gain by finding someone to fence it once they mine the information they need. Doubtless, someone will see the value in 80 million "fullz," the term of art in identity theft circles for all the personally identifiable information needed to scam someone.

The Anthem breach revealed a more profound problem, too, and even the people who are supposed to know the score don't seem to understand it. This was painfully obvious when Anthem's CEO pointed to the hackers' failure to get health records, credit card numbers, or financial data in the breach. While it's clear he was trying to cast the best possible light on a nightmare scenario, he couldn't have been more incorrect about the gravitas of the situation. The information that the hackers got was a very big deal. Those fullz included names, physical and email addresses, birthdates, medical IDs, phone numbers, and employment information—a treasure trove for the cyberpirates of identity theft.

One of the many reasons that the identity theft epidemic keeps getting worse is a lack of public knowledge. It's telling that the leader of a huge organization like Anthem did not understand the seriousness of so many email addresses being exposed. This kind of ignorance would be shocking if it weren't for the fact that we see it every day in the news and in enterprise communications. What *is* shocking is that Anthem's CEO made these comments even while knowing that another piece of his clients' information was stolen, an even more important piece—Social Security numbers.

Often what's lacking in the aftermath of these breaches is a calm voice delivering the bad news. So here it is: With your Social Security number in the wind, whoever finds it—or, more likely, whoever buys it on one of the many black-market information exchanges on the deep web—holds the keys to *every* part of your life. What

---

Email Is Better than Explosives

One of the biggest bank heist operations in history—in which over a billion dollars may have been stolen in more than thirty countries—was perpetrated by the Carbanak gang with a simple spearphishing scheme.

They gained access to bank computers and learned how they worked. Then they took a withdrawal from the vaults. No dynamite needed.

that means—plain and simple—is that you're going to need an efficient way to keep one eye over your shoulder, all the time.

While Anthem got out in front of the breach faster than any of the larger companies breached in recent years, they were far from perfect. Congressional committees have correctly noted that Anthem took more than a month to notify the members that were on the breached databases. While they should be commended for the speed of their public disclosure, they did an abysmal job of explaining what was at stake, why the breach mattered, and how it could affect individuals. In other words, when it came time to let their customers know what it all meant—that their personally identifiable information was a commodity that would most likely be sold to a crime ring or lone criminal who would use it to defraud them—Anthem was a no-show. Whether or not that was a public relations move, I cannot say, but it definitely wasn't solution minded.

Here's what Anthem should have said: Everything a criminal might need to obtain medical treatment, devices, or medications in an Anthem customer's name—tainting their medical files with information that could lead a doctor to choose the wrong treatment or even make deadly decisions—was out there in the world for anyone to abuse. Every single person whose PII was leaked in the Anthem breach is a single act of fraud away from having a medical file become a murder weapon.

Death by Medical Identity Theft

Whether healthcare fraud is committed to get lifesaving treatment, cosmetic surgery, or medicine for erectile dysfunction, there's a good chance the "fake you" isn't your blood type. Or maybe they can take penicillin, but you're allergic to it. When your medical file gets comingled with someone else's, the results can be deadly.

Just as easily, fraudulent tax returns (using their name, date of birth, Social Security number, and a fake W-2) can divert refunds to a scammer. Anyone can obtain personal loans, credit cards, and mortgages using an Anthem customer's credit profile, accessed with information compromised in the breach; the same data could be used to obtain fake papers for undocumented workers to get jobs, with the income being reported to federal and state tax authorities under a breach victim's Social Security number. The children of breach victims were exposed as well—their identities are now vulnerable. The list of crimes that can be committed while leaving a trail of breadcrumbs back to a breach victim is endless.

> $5.8 billion of fraudulent returns were stolen in 2014. The IRS estimates tax fraud will increase to $21 billion by 2016.

Seemingly every aspect of our lives has been affected. The same week that the Anthem attack made headlines, the software giant Intuit shut down the state tax filing option on TurboTax for almost a day after detecting a large number of fraudulent filings. There was fallout all over the country. In Minnesota, no TurboTax e-filings were accepted. Both Alabama and Utah took a mellower approach, issuing taxpayer warnings. The state of Vermont stopped all refunds. And here's the kicker: There wasn't even a breach, at least that we are aware of. A stampede of identity thieves started e-filing with other people's information, attempting to divert millions of dollars in refunds, and the only way to stop them was to shut down TurboTax. Whoever was behind the attack was using the kind of information that was leaked in the Anthem breach and countless other compromises over the past decade. First, the good news. All affected parties did a good job, or at least better than we might have expected a few years ago. They saw something was amiss, and they took action—although they were criticized for moving too slowly, and there are allegations that they knowingly allowed bad returns to flow through to the IRS.

It may sound implausible that so many fraudulent tax forms could be arriving without a single breach, but it isn't. There is no way to visualize how much data has been stolen. I can't tell you how many times I've watched people's jaws drop when I tell them that the black market information exchange has operations that are so organized that a criminal can call a help line for technical support or to request a refund.

A staggering amount of data liberated by breaches, scams, social network oversharing, and individual compromise has been aggregated, and those blocks of identity-rich information are for sale every day. Tax fraud is just one manifestation of that reality. Almost any ill-gotten gain can be had with the right combination of sensitive information and bravado.

We're all at risk because we are still in the Wild West days of electronic personal information and commerce. The fact that organizations don't encrypt the PII they gather and store is inexcusable. It's a serious problem when a sitting governor, South Carolina's Nikki Haley, can say, "A lot of banks don't encrypt. It's very complicated. It's very cumbersome. There's a lot of numbers involved with it." It's the sort of attitude that explains her government's failure to encrypt a breached database containing the tax information of every citizen in her state. But the "encryption is hard" dog just doesn't hunt when it comes to public perception of the problem these days. Of course, South Carolina is not alone. A recent Government Accountability Office report confirms that a significant percentage of federal agencies are not secure. Too many businesses and institutions have yet to harden their defenses or encrypt their data, even after they have suffered a breach. Given all this, consumers are starting to understand that we are on our own—and how scary that can be.

At a March 2015 event in Washington, DC, sponsored by the Identity Theft Resource Center, keynoter Terrell McSweeny, one of five members of the Federal Trade Commission, said in reference to a 2014 Gallup poll, "Americans were more concerned about ID theft than violent crime, natural disasters, or terrorism. 69 percent of Americans said they were very concerned about the safety of their credit cards, and 62 percent had similar worries about their smart phones and computers."

We live in a very connected world where convenience increasingly trumps security—often in the name of innovation and whizbang. We've also learned the hard way that no system is more secure than its weakest link, and humans are almost always the weakest link. Bad practices and lousy data hygiene are about as common as flies in a feedlot on a hot summer day. There is no segment of the connected world that isn't complicit in the problem. When the Ponemon Institute conducted a survey of nearly one hundred medical providers in early 2014, 88 percent said that they allowed doctors and other medical professionals to connect personal devices to their secure systems, even though those personal smartphones and laptops could contain all manner of viruses or malware. Of all the people who might grok the concept of contagion, you'd think doctors might. But the report suggests that most had no issue with healthcare professionals connecting their who-knows-where-they've-been computers to a secure system. More than 50 percent of respondents said that this practice raised serious security concerns, but only 38 percent said they were planning to do anything about it.

> In the open market of personally identifiable information and bad enterprise privacy practices, only you can know if you're all right.

One might hope that Congress would be taking some action to solve this problem. At least three administrations and scores of federal legislators have talked about doing something meaningful in the areas of privacy, cybersecurity, and identity theft, yet we don't have much to show for it. More recently, through an executive order and a State of the Union address, President Obama put those issues squarely into the spotlight.

For now, we have to accept the bipartisan talking point that, as I've put it on various occasions, "we are seeing momentum" toward a solution to the identity theft problem. But lest we forget, we are also seeing countless data breaches and identity thefts, which is where you come into the picture. If you don't get what I'm saying here, stand in front of a mirror. There's the enemy. Swiping doesn't happen to you. You swipe your own information all the time. You're in a system that runs on information, and no amount of wishful thinking or semantics is going to extricate you. No one is blameless here. If you're unclear on where you're "going wrong," think about it in different terms. We all need to take responsibility for the attackable surface, or vulnerability, of our personal information and our areas of exposure. Depending on what we do, and how we do it, those areas become bigger or smaller targets.

Here's a thumbnail. We expose our most sensitive personal information any time we

- pick up a phone, respond to a text, click on a link, or carelessly provide personal information to someone we don't know;
- fail to properly secure computers or mobile devices (smartphones, tablets, or laptops);
- create easy-to-crack passwords;
- discard, rather than shred, a document that contains PII;
- respond to an email that directs us to call a number we can't independently confirm, or complete an attachment that asks for our PII in an insecure environment;
- save our user ID or password on a website or in an app as a shortcut for future logins;
- use the same user ID or password throughout our financial, social networking, and email universes;
- take quizzes that subtly ask for information we've provided as the answers to security questions on various websites;

- snap pictures with our smartphone or digital camera without disabling the geotagging function;
- fail to replace a manufacturer's default password with a long and strong one of our own on any connected appliance or electronic device that we put in our homes;
- use our email address as a user name/ID, if we have the option to change it;
- use simple PINs like 1234 or 9876 or a birthday;
- forget to obtain, review, and correct our credit reports;
- go twenty-four hours without reviewing our bank and credit card accounts to make absolutely sure that every transaction we see is familiar;
- fail to enroll in free transactional monitoring programs offered by banks, credit unions, and credit card providers that notify us every time there is any activity in our accounts;
- use a free Wi-Fi network, without confirming it is correctly identified and secure, to check email or access financial services websites that contain our sensitive data.

In each of these instances, we leave ourselves vulnerable to those who consider the theft of our identity as their day job. In the big picture, worst-case scenario, we may even be contributing our personal data to state-sponsored hackers or hacktivists planning the equivalent of a "denial of service" attack on our economy, for instance by freezing everyone's bank accounts at the same time.

The bottom line is that we're all in this together. In this ever-evolving, connected world, it's impossible to duck, bob, or weave your way past the bad guys. Even proactive measures to protect your identity like monitoring your credit regularly, setting up transaction alerts, or freezing your credit are no guarantee that your identity won't be stolen or used in a way that won't show up on your credit report right away, or in some instances won't be at all apparent, such as medical identity theft. But the more you know and monitor, and the more you get out in front of the possibility that you may have or will become the victim of a fraudster, the quicker things will get back to normal for you when your information is used.

It should go without saying that governments and businesses should have to protect our PII by law, and if they fail to do their duty, they should be held accountable. That said, each of us has a responsibility to minimize our risk of exposure, to be as alert as possible to signs of an identity-related problem, and to have a damage-control program to put ourselves back together in the event we are compromised.

PART 2
The Basics of What You Can Do

4

Understanding the Problem
Is the Solution

When it comes to data security and the real-life impact of identity theft, public awareness is at an all-time high. But there is still great confusion and ignorance about what it is, how it happens, and what can be done to avoid the pitfalls of life after a data breach or a personal compromise.

Most of us still feel flummoxed—and perhaps a bit panicked—when something does happen. Even if it's a situation that can be easily remedied, like a compromised credit card, where the problem is relatively small. Even if the only real life consequences are a day or two's wait for a replacement card and the need to notify a few creditors that your billing information has changed, you feel violated. You wonder if it's going to happen again. And depending upon the source of the compromise, it may well happen again. So you stew and wonder some more.

The unfortunate part is that identity thieves understand this. In the mad dash to understand the full ramifications of what's happened to you, you may expose yourself to further trouble—for instance by providing your information to phony resolution "experts," only to be guided through a process that brings about further compromise by the very data wolves in sheep's clothing who ran the scam in the first place, offering a helping hand while the other hand empties what's left in the victim's pockets.

Taking a few simple steps will help you avoid crooked "helpers" like these and more generally minimize your panic. Instead, you'll make a proactive decision to change the way you conduct your affairs going forward. If you do this in earnest, your life will never come to a grinding halt as a result of data-related crime again.

> In the disorienting world that confronts the newly compromised, it is exceedingly difficult to know who to trust.

If you don't subscribe to an identity theft resolution service and lack a plan of action before you suffer a personal compromise (other than the theft of a payment card, which can be solved with a couple of phone calls), you will need to spend more time and more money than you are probably prepared to spend. Then, after you have worked your way through the maze of law enforcement, credit bureau, creditor, and record-keeping requirements necessary to put yourself back together again, you will almost assuredly spend additional time—more than you thought humanly possible—rearranging the way you make your information available both online and in your everyday transactions.

For this to really work, you need to be willing to make a few adjustments in the way you approach your identity and your data hygiene.

What the great majority of current and future identity theft victims fail to understand is that they really must be their own first line of defense. Since identity thieves can't realistically be completely stopped, you can instead focus on making yourself a harder target, and be more ready when the attack comes.

While it may seem a shade shy of an identity theft silver bullet, protecting yourself in this new age requires a paradigm shift in the way we think about our personal information. It's doubtful that the stats on identity-related crime are going to markedly improve any time soon.

For starters, law enforcement can only do so much for you. Yes, you're required to file a police report, but that's only one piece of the puzzle. It's their job to catch the bad guys, but they cannot protect your data, and it's not their mission to help you return to economic or reputational normalcy.

What's missing is a cultural change, which isn't going to happen anytime soon. The shift I'm talking about involves the way data is stored at the enterprise level, but more than that, it's about the way people are taught to handle personal information. The ultimate guardian of the consumer is the consumer.

If you want to better protect yourself from the ravages of identity theft, you need to understand who identity thieves are. Try to be aware of what you do and how your choices make you more or less vulnerable.

> Data hygiene should be as much a part of life-skills education as cooking an egg and sewing on a button.

A simple practice like shredding your personal documents can help, but it's not a solution. Identity thieves can be anyone from a dental hygienist pilfering patient files to small-time crooks breaking into mailboxes or stealing unshredded garbage or tax-related documents during filing season. But when it comes to international

---

Forgotten Files

Remember that late-night trip to a regional hospital for stitches, where you hurriedly filled out a form providing both your Social Security number and your insurance information? How did they store it?

Imagine all the metal filing cabinets in the world—or even just the ones in your hometown—containing some of your personal information. Now ask yourself a simple question: Are all of them locked? Bonus question: How hard is it to break a lock?

crime syndicates that breach the databases of multi-billion-dollar multinational corporations and sell the liberated information, deploying a paper shredder is like bringing a knife to a gunfight.

Here's an example of a small case in the larger criminal eco-system of identity theft. Two men were arrested in Lowndes County, Georgia, after a routine traffic stop enabled an alert law enforcement officer to spot the telltale signs of identity theft. According to an online account, "Deputies found a notebook with names, birthdays, and social security numbers of over 70 different people. They also found twenty credit cards that had been encoded with stolen information." A shredder couldn't have stopped these guys, because they almost certainly didn't find all the information they needed to set up those phony credit cards in a Dumpster. They may have friended their marks on Facebook, used Google searches, scoured public databases, or accessed poorly secured private ones. They may have even rifled through public documents. There are numerous possibilities, but the most likely scenario is that the DNA of those counterfeit credit cards was magnetic stripe data pilfered by skimmers within credit card readers, or sensitive personal information snatched from a breached database that was bought on the cybercrime black market.

You Are an Identity Thief's Day Job

Like it or not, your information is out there. Cobbling together enough of it to commit identity theft is a full-time job for tens of thousands of criminals.

For a price ranging from $1 for a credit card number with a name, expiration date, and security code to $500 for a fullz, anyone can be in business. And a whole lot of people are. With the geometric increases in data-related crimes, it is clear that new fraudsters are minted every day.

Even if your sensitive information wasn't sitting in one of the approximately 1 billion files that have been compromised in breaches over the past few years, it may be available on a number of deep web sites that hawk pieces of stolen identities.

It doesn't take much. With a name and date of birth or email address, or user ID and password, or a correlation between a name and an address, an identity thief with a tad of persistence can start piecing together enough factoids about you to become you in the eyes of a creditor. It's enough to get approval for a mortgage, an auto loan, or financing that can be utilized to buy just about anything.

Who or what is an identity thief? He or she can be an "it" or a "they"—a boiler room filled with people working the seams of your information goldmine, a lone hacker, a neighbor, a home healthcare worker, a medical professional, or even—in one infamous case—your mother. An alarming number of fraudsters prey on friends and family. It can be literally anyone who knows you—especially those whom you might not count as friends but who have access to your home or your office.

This new breed of criminal often operates in plain sight. The tools of their trade—a phone and a computer—are the same as anyone with an office job. Larger identity theft operations buy breached information in huge lots, while smaller rackets and individual contractors go on scavenger hunts. They are looking for tidbits of data, including personal history and behaviors, that can provide clues to security questions and answers, passwords, or whatever else they need to help them get what they're after. The information is scattered across public-facing websites and vulnerable digital caches located on servers that are breached daily due to uploaded malware, human error, and rogue employees. Identity thieves are looking for information stored in filing cabinets at offices with lax security. They intently watch as we plant the seeds of our own undoing on social media sites: one tag, comment, or tweet at a time.

These criminals inflict far more damage on their victims than simply buying cars and opening lines of credit. They target children

The Deep Web or the Dark Web?

The deep web is a hidden part of the Internet. It consists of a vast number of sites, most of them thoroughly boring, that can't be found by a traditional search engine like Google. To access these sites, you need a password, a specific URL, a sophisticated understanding of how computers communicate, or sometimes all of the above. The deep web is four hundred to six hundred times larger than the "surface web," that is, the familiar sites you can access via search engines and see every day.

Although there is popular confusion on this point, the deep web is not a meeting place for criminals. That's the dark web, where an enormous amount of the content is illegal, a significant percentage of it child pornography or otherwise sinister material (like how to build a bomb). While the dark web is something most web surfers can't find on their own—and wouldn't want to anyway—the deep web is of less concern: it's simply a part of the Internet that is not indexed by search engines—password-protected sites, dynamic pages, and encrypted networks. Additionally, much of the content on the deep web has little to no value for an identity thief, and consists of proprietary material and countless pages that are neither intended for public consumption nor even remotely interesting to anyone without a sophisticated technology background. However, there are plenty of instances of cyber sleuths finding PII on non-indexed sites. The only thing that makes it part of the deep web is that it's not findable. However, there is plenty of illegal content out there. It is on the dark web—tucked away in a vast sea of obscenity—that the marketplace for your personal information exists.

in foster care—many of them at risk—and destroy their credit before they're even old enough to use it. They're intentionally attaching bad debt to the good names of unsuspecting victims. They're infecting personal computers, work stations, and networks of servers—demanding ransom at penalty of destroying systems, deleting files, and releasing embarrassing personal information or intellectual property. They're buying medical devices, obtaining medical services, and acquiring prescriptions on the dimes of millions of unsuspecting victims or by way of co-opted medical insurance. They are entering into fraudulent arrangements with shady doctors.

These days, toddlers are awakened in the middle of the night by sociopaths screaming expletives through hacked baby monitors; young people are learning more than a decade after the fact that they can't buy a car or rent an apartment because their credit has been decimated; star-crossed romantics are falling in love with—and sending money to—people they've never met; and cash-strapped taxpayers are waiting anxiously for refunds that get diverted to fraudsters who filed fake returns with doctored W-2s literally hours after tax season had begun. Identity theft victims get arrested for crimes they didn't commit. They land on no-fly lists. They are denied employment because their credit report says they can't be trusted. They are at risk of injury or death as they lay on stretchers in emergency rooms because their medical files have been compromised. Their health information has been comingled with that of an identity thief or his customer, causing their blood type to change, or the erasure or deletion of life-threatening allergies. Today's identity thieves are persistent. They don't work on the clock. And they have a highly evolved ecosystem. Regardless of who you are, what you do, or where you live. To them you look like a million bucks—or at least a few thousand.

Identity thieves are high tech and extremely ambitious. With a single scam, they can easily rake in millions of dollars. For example, there was a scam that surfaced in 2014, in which unexplained credit card charges for $9.84 appeared on millions of accounts throughout the country—and one has to assume that it resulted in a multimillion-dollar haul. Larger operations even offer help lines for thieves to contact in the event any stolen payment card numbers are found to be incorrect, or if accounts have been closed or replaced by victims or financial institutions before being converted into counterfeit cards and fraudulent charges. Then there are hackers who provide 800 numbers staffed around the clock by customer service representatives to help victimized consumers pay the ransom to decrypt their own hijacked files. How 'bout them apples?

Identity theft is a growth industry, which means it attracts highly intelligent and hardworking people. The most successful fraudsters are top-flight innovators. Their levels of relentlessness, sophistication, and creativity parallel those of the best of the best at Apple and Google. These guys make a killing, and they're not looking for stock options. For them, it's all about hacking for dollars, and they love what they do.

That's why monitoring the various aspects of your financial life to make sure you're not a victim is a necessary daily activity. In fact, logging on to your credit card and bank accounts—all of them—every day shouldn't be viewed as a chore. It's a privilege. Take it as an opportunity to be like Scrooge McDuck, taking a daily swim in your tower filled with gold doubloons. Remember—not everyone is so lucky!

After getting yourself into the right frame of mind and creating a personal monitoring plan to help you peruse the various websites that provide a snapshot of the state of your affairs—which might require a couple hours of your time initially—it really doesn't take long to stay on top of your credit and identity profile. Your goal here: Get acquainted with your attackable surface.

Self-monitoring doesn't necessarily need to be a round-the-clock process, either. Once a day is more than adequate. Think of identity thieves as the more familiar kinds of muggers and crooks. How would you conduct yourself if you got lost in a rough part of town? Would you be careful? Would you stay a little more aware of your surroundings? The deep web, and the modern world more generally, is that rough part of town. So be vigilant. Self-monitoring should become as natural as looking both ways before you cross the street.

Your mission is to make monitoring your identity a seamless part of your routine. Like the traffic you encounter at rush hour or the line you wait in to get coffee, it's just another thing in the order of operations of your day-to-day personal math.

Many of us spend a fair amount of time on social media. In the face of overwhelming evidence to the contrary, most of us post and tweet and reblog as if we were invincible to fraud. I'm by no means saying you have to exempt yourself from social media. I think it's great. But remember—everything you put out there can be used to identify you. Remember the *Science Magazine* study we looked at in Chapter 1? Here was its conclusion: The more time you spend on social media, the greater your vulnerability to hacking. Every picture you post, every quiz question you answer, every experience you recount, every shred of personal information you willingly share with "friends" increases the area of your attackable surface.

> Check your accounts and personal data security, then keep it in mind as you go about your day.

People who don't have your best interests at heart scan your posts daily, looking for opportunities. They have a huge repertoire of crimes that they can commit. Unless you have disabled the location function of your digital device, or your favorite social networking site uses a geotag scrambler when you upload your personal photographs, sophisticated hackers can figure out where you took the shot. Think about how many photos you have taken in or around your home, proudly showing off your new car, cuddly new pet, blazing fast Alienware laptop, or valuable painting. Thieves need only wait for you to leave for work, or to go on vacation and share your travel adventures in real time on Facebook, Instagram, and Twitter, to know when to break into your home.

Getting up to speed on the essential dos and don'ts of social media, including how to master privacy settings or how to spot a spearfishing email, is a huge step in the right direction. Take a breath before clicking on a link in an email sent by your BFF. Learn about the privacy settings on your Twitter app, your smartphone camera, and your laptop. And think twice before clicking if something about an email seems odd.

Minimizing your exposure is the other essential. Every Internet-connected device you own is a point of vulnerability, so master them all. Today, everything from appliances to cars to computers and smartphones is yoked together, and with each additional acquisition your attackable surface grows. If you always pay in cash and live completely off the grid, you're less exposed than someone living in a smart home. Chances are good you fall somewhere between these two extremes. Get to know which devices in your home are connected to the Internet, and learn what kinds of information they share.

You need to learn how to avoid the Identity Theft Darwin Awards. You may not be able to stop identity thieves, but you can avoid being an easy target. Use long and strong passwords, change them regularly, and do not share them throughout your digital universe of email, retail, financial, and social accounts. Use a virtual private network (VPN) or secure network. Stay information agile.

The Bellwether Gets Away

Like that old joke about the two guys getting chased by a bear in the woods—you don't have to be able to outrun the bear, you just need to be faster than the guy next to you.

Identity thieves look for victims who will stay victims for a long time because they are oblivious to the damage being done to them. Meanwhile, fraudsters have only one objective: Open as many credit cards as possible, buy as many cars and tickets to exotic destinations as they can, and maybe even pay for a little cosmetic surgery before you notice, or are noticed by a debt collector for a bill you never received from a company with which you have never done any business.

There is a simple way to avoid getting gutted by these information termites. It is neither hard to do, nor terribly time consuming. Here's what you do: Keep an eye on them. And by them, I mean not only your financial accounts, your credit report, and your credit scores. I mean the bad guys, too.

You are probably beginning to see the parallel here to the management of your personal finances. That's the key to efficiently and effectively managing your identity. You know what you can spend, and where to draw the lines to maximize your buying power by using credit wisely (and if you don't, keep reading for a thumbnail of how to do that). The same rules apply when it comes to the sort of things that can go wrong if somebody starts utilizing your personal information. Knowing your basic credit obligations and expenditures on any given day at a glance, you are in a unique position to monitor your accounts with minimal effort. No one can do it as expediently as you. When you see a scam right away, you can better contain the damage. For instance, if you check your credit card accounts daily, you will see pending charges that have not yet been approved, which gives you plenty of time to alert your credit card company that there's been a fraud. The card number is deactivated, and the thief is out of business . . . momentarily—he or she may have a bandolier filled with cards. If you monitor your credit reports frequently, work with companies that provide continuing access to free credit scores that are updated monthly, put fraud alerts on your accounts, and, where appropriate, freeze your credit, the same thing will happen with bigger ticket items—like cars, lines of credit, and mortgages— that require a Social Security number to get approved. If you limit the ability of a thief to use your Social Security number in that way, your Social Security number will wind up marked "not worth the trouble."

> Minimize, monitor, and manage the damage. Identity theft cannot be prevented, but it can be contained. Be paranoid! Be ready!

We are living in a postprivacy world. We knowingly overshare and unknowingly are tracked by thousands of organizations from the NSA to our favorite retailers to data brokers we have neither heard of nor agreed to give our information to. It's important to bear in mind throughout your day that over 1 billion files containing every stripe of sensitive personal information have been improperly accessed by people who want to exploit it for their personal gain, and the pace of the identity insecurity meltdown is quickening.

While there are regulations and government standards on the horizon—including federal protections and guarantees—it doesn't matter how many laws there are or how vigorously they are enforced, because the whole constellation of what comprises the current threat is too gargantuan to be regulated out of existence. The attackable surface is too vast. When it comes to the threat of identity-related fraud, the consumer is his or her own first and last line of defense. No one has a stake in our financial security more than we do, and no one is more familiar with our financial transactions than we are. As detailed in the next chapter, that's why it is critical for us all to adopt a culture of minimizing exposure, monitoring our accounts, and controlling the damage. There is no substitute for understanding the risks, being aware, and knowing what to do or where to go for help. While an educated consumer undoubtedly will experience some form of identity-related crime, they are going to sleep better at night knowing they've taken the proper steps and that there are solutions.

5

The Three Ms

No one ever thinks they are going to be targeted by hackers looking for that big score. I call it "The Other Guy" syndrome. But, of course, to everyone in the world except you, you're The Other Guy.

So what should you do?

I call my strategy the Three Ms:

1. Minimize your exposure
2. Monitor your accounts
3. Manage the damage

It sounds simple, but I promise if you do these three things, your life will be a lot less painful when the inevitable happens and you get got.

Minimize Your Exposure

This is probably the most familiar of the Three Ms. Don't share too much information with folks you don't know—whether in person, on the phone, or online via social media. Make sure that you set long and strong passwords; properly secure all computers, smartphones, and tablets used by you and your family; use two-factor authentication where possible; and shred sensitive documents. This is a good start.

In fact, my friends at the nonprofit Identity Theft Resource Center (ITRC) in San Diego, California, a wonderful volunteer organization that has helped tens of thousands of victims deal with the nightmare of identity theft and educated millions more, start with a similar set of protocols. They call it SHRED:

- **S**trengthen passwords
- **H**andle PII with care
- **R**ead credit reports annually
- **E**mpty your purse/wallet
- **D**iscuss these tips with friends

I encourage you to do all of these things. But you also need to see the big picture. So here's the task entire: Change the way you think about identity theft and your personally identifiable information. Minimizing your exposure to identity theft in large part is a matter of educating yourself about the many dangers out there.

The result will be gradual but unmistakable.

You will naturally become infinitely more vigilant. You will learn what happens when you overshare on social media. You will be careful about who you tell what and why. You will think in terms of what could happen before you dive for what you want to have happen in the moment. You will not let down your guard.

There are of course a number of companies out there that say they can protect you, but if you listen closely, none of them say they can prevent identity theft. Over the years, several have tried to persuade consumers that they can prevent it altogether. But the Federal Trade Commission (FTC) wasn't buying any of that. Nor was the Consumer Federation of America (CFA). Because the fact of the matter is that they can't. If you find yourself tempted by an offer from a company that promises to prevent identity theft from happening to you, don't take the plunge. No reputable company will ever make such representations. For a treasure trove of information about how to intelligently choose an identity theft services provider, go to the CFA-sponsored site: www.idtheftinfo.org.

Monitor Your Accounts

Once you're in the habit of minimizing your exposure, the name of the game is vigilance. First, you need to check your credit. Once a year, you can get a copy of your credit reports from each of the three major credit reporting agencies, for no fee, at www .AnnualCreditReport.com.

Next, enroll in transactional notification programs. You will find that they may be offered for free through your bank, credit union, and credit card issuers. Alternately, you can subscribe to various credit and fraud monitoring services that will inform you of any changes to your credit report—like new accounts or inquiries that might indicate someone is trying to open a fraudulent account in your name. Depending on the service you select, you can set your security protocols so tightly that a new line of credit cannot be opened at all because no one, including you, can gain access, or you can set it up so there can be no green light until you receive and respond to an instant or slightly delayed alert that someone has tried to create a new account. Alternately, you can set the alert loosely so that you simply receive notice when activity in excess of a preset dollar amount occurs in any of your existing financial accounts.

It may seem like a nuisance to field an email or text or app notification every time you buy something with your credit or debit card, but you'll be glad you activated those notifications the day you get one about a purchase you didn't make or the creation of an account for which you never applied.

Fraud alerts are another option to consider.

The three reporting agencies offer initial fraud alert services, extended fraud alerts, and active duty military alerts. If you already subscribe to a credit monitoring service, fraud alerts may be an inexpensive add-on. There are also services that allow you to monitor your children's Social Security numbers for signs of identity theft.

A credit freeze is a more comprehensive shield, but it is more cumbersome than a fraud alert, and it's still not fail-safe. Once activated, no one—including you—can access your credit for the purpose of opening new accounts. To allow access, you must use a special PIN (or password) to thaw the freeze. To initiate a freeze, you must sign up with all three bureaus individually, and there are costs associated with both freezing and thawing accounts unless you are a senior citizen or an identity theft victim. Unfortunately, the freeze doesn't stop people from taking over your existing accounts. It doesn't prevent criminals from committing tax fraud, child identity theft, medical identity theft, or criminal identity theft. And it can be worked around by presenting two forms of ID and a utility bill, as well as completely eliminated by an identity thief who has gained access to all of your PII and the ability to decipher your PIN or password.

Manage the Damage

So, how bad will it be if or when your identity is stolen? In many cases, far worse than you can imagine, because identity thieves do the unimaginable. This is why it is very important to pick a reputable company that offers a range of high-touch services. The good news here is that you may discover that an organization with which you already have a relationship—perhaps your insurance carrier, financial services provider, or employer—offers a product or provides access to a professional service that will help you navigate the rocky shoals of whatever identity-related issue you are facing. Check to see if any company or institution with which you are doing business can provide you with identity theft resolution or identity management products and services, since it may cost you little or nothing, and you may even find out that you are already under their protection. While peace of mind is worth a great deal, it's even nicer when it comes free of charge.

The key to properly practicing the Three Ms is engagement. Your only hope of quickly detecting victimization and effectively containing the nightmare of identity theft is to stay engaged and invested in the process. And, beyond question, it is a process that must be practiced daily. (That means you really have to do it.) The goal of a shred-a-thon is peace of mind, but a false sense of security is in no one's best interest. Real peace of mind comes with real knowledge and concrete action.

> **Reality Check**
>
> Hackers will always attack the weakest link. If they determine that the big guys have toughened up, they're just going to go after easier targets, like individuals and small businesses. If there's a thief in the neighborhood, they'll look for the house with no guard dog.

Here are a few practical steps you can take to make each of the Three Ms happen for yourself.

Minimize Your Exposure

The most important step you can take is to be proactive about your own security, rather than waiting until it's breached. Some specific steps include the following:

- Never carry your Social Security card, or those of your children, in your purse or your wallet.
- Never carry your Medicare card if you can avoid it. If you must, make a copy, redact all numbers but the last four, and black out the letter. If the medical provider asks for your number, provide it.

- Limit the amount of credit and debit cards you carry and keep a list of all payment cards and toll-free numbers for the issuers in a safe place. Also, always have at least one credit and one debit card in reserve so that you can use them while waiting for replacements to arrive.
- Make sure all the computers in your home have the latest antivirus and malware protection programs and that the security software is updated regularly. (It is best if they do automatic updates.)
- Secure your smart phones with PINs that are not easily decipherable, use long and strong passwords on every account, and never save a user ID or password in any app on any device.
- Never share user IDs or passwords over email, social networks, or other digital accounts.
- Create a special email account for online shopping and the aggregation of receipts.
- Talk to your family about the need for security. Make sure everyone is acquainted with common modes of attack: phishing and spearphishing emails, vishing and smishing (all of these terms are explained in Appendix 2 at the end of this book), plus the various kinds of malware out there and the perils of oversharing on social media sites. Get them in the habit of securing or turning off devices that aren't being used.
- Limit access to sensitive information and accounts to the adults who handle them, and, if at all possible, only access these files and accounts on a computer that is password protected and "off-limits" to the rest of the household.
- Never authenticate yourself to anyone who contacts you in person, by phone, or online and asks you to confirm that you are you. Only provide authentication information if you have initiated the contact and they need to verify your identity for your protection.

- When dealing with a social networking environment, set privacy controls tightly and be aware that privacy policies change frequently, requiring you to constantly review terms and conditions and adjust your privacy settings accordingly. Never take quizzes online, because the customary information gathered could well be answers to security questions that prove who you are. Do not overshare information with people who may well not be your friends but rather cyber cat burglars who are looking to steal your PII and then exploit it for their gain.
- Every time you buy an electronic device or appliance for your home that will be connected by router or Wi-Fi to the Internet, read the disclosures, follow the instructions, and change the default password to a long and strong one of your choosing.
- Enroll in, or activate, two-factor authentication everywhere you can.
- Make sure you have the right physical security for your home or business.
- Securely store all documents containing personal identifying information and shred them when you no longer need them.
- Always make sure to destroy any documents or hard drives you no longer use.
- Check yourself. Are you are as safe as you think you are? Security measures that were good enough last week may no longer do the trick.

Monitor Your Security

- Sign up for transactional monitoring programs offered by your bank, credit union, and credit card company.
- Check to see if any of the insurance carrier or financial services institutions you do business with offers free or

discounted access to monitoring services, and if so, use them.

- Check your credit report at least once a year. At www.annualcreditreport.com you are entitled to one free copy from each of the three national credit reporting agencies (Experian, Equifax, and TransUnion). While many people get all three at once, others get one every four months so that they can see three different snapshots of their credit during the year. Consider paying for access to a monthly (or more frequently updated) report from one or all three of the credit reporting agencies.
- Enroll in programs that allow you to access your credit scores at least every thirty days.
- Consider purchasing more sophisticated and robust credit and fraud monitoring services. You should look in particular for those organizations that offer identity theft recovery services as well as monitoring. Always read the details of any monitoring offer to make sure you fully understand what you are buying.
- Check your bank accounts daily.
- Check your credit accounts daily.

Manage the Damage

Have a plan before you have an issue. This may include the following:

- Keep a list of companies, credit accounts, bank accounts, and other places you do business with so that if you are victimized you have a reference sheet to use.
- Contact your insurance agent or financial institution to see if they offer cyber liability or identity protection coverage, or an identity theft damage control program. You may be pleasantly surprised to learn that you are already

protected. If not, find out what, if anything, they offer; what you need to do to enroll; whether it is free; and, if not, what the cost is.

- The alternative is to do everything yourself. It requires enormous discipline and nerves of steel. It is time consuming, emotionally draining, and may not yield the desired result. The practical issue is that with identity theft, even in our more enlightened state, the victim quickly discovers that he or she is guilty until proven innocent.

PART 3
The Many Types of Identity Theft

6

Spies in Your Home

*How the Internet of Things May Violate
Your Privacy, Threaten Your Security,
and Ruin Your Credit*

In 2015, somewhere in the neighborhood of 1 billion Internet of Things (IoT) devices will be purchased, an increase of 60 percent over the previous year. Next year will be even bigger: By the time 2016 rolls around, there will be around 3 billion IoT devices in use across the nation.

A couple of years ago, a survey found that three out of four Americans had no clue that there was such an animal as the Internet of Things, and many likely still don't know. But the IoT has arrived, and it's only getting bigger, so it's best to get a handle on what it means.

The IoT can be any product or appliance equipped with a chip for storing data and web connectivity. The point is two-fold: service and data collection. Whether we're talking about a car or a dishwasher, manufacturers can identify this or that "thing" by a unique code, then send it information over the Internet, including commands and software updates; conversely, they can also receive communications from it. Many of the devices that fall under the IoT heading have web- and app-based interfaces that allow end users to control them from wherever they may be, whether it is a security camera, a front door, or a clothes dryer.

Frequently, these souped-up appliances are marketed as "smart devices," and they have a variety of benefits. A smart coffee machine can make your coffee at 7:30 every morning, or smart tech can warm up your car whenever the temperature is below freezing. It can open the doors at your business and turn on the lights. The possibilities are endless, and excruciatingly cool. But the downside, of course, is the security risk. Because this data is moving around on devices that are not universally protected, in an environment where there is no established security standard, we have no way of assessing the level of risk.

Most IoT products are often woefully underprotected (or not protected at all), and that opens the door to hacking. From the criminal's perspective, the IoT is, simply, an opportunity—a bunch of holes in the fence of your information security. It expands your attackable surface. Computer manufacturers and software companies devote attention and resources to providing security, but appliance makers have little understanding of the field. It is only a matter of time before the hackers start digging into their programs.

In fact, the first proven large-scale hack of IoT devices occurred in December 2013 and the first week of 2014, according to the security-as-a-service company Proofpoint, based in Sunnyvale, California. The company's press release detailed the marshaling of conventional household smart, or IoT, appliances. "The global attack campaign involved more than 750,000 malicious email communications coming from more than 100,000 everyday consumer gadgets such as home-networking routers, connected multi-media centers, televisions and at least one refrigerator that had been compromised and used as a platform to launch attacks."

Normally, a mass of spam as large as 750,000 emails would be caught by filters. But what if the filters didn't know the emails were coming from the same place? In this attack, which took place between December 23, 2013, and January 6, 2014, bursts of email—as many as 100,000 of them at a time—were sent out through an army of machines several times a day. Twenty-five per-cent of the email was sent via noncomputer "things" (i.e., not a laptop, desktop computer, or smartphone). Because each IP address was programmed by the hackers to send no more

> Are you sure you wouldn't prefer a dumb appliance? Don't forget: Only smart things can plot against you.

than ten emails, none of the location-based defenses that networks use to block spam were triggered. After all, who would suspect a refrigerator of malfeasance?

Samsung Privacy Policy—SmartTV Supplement

Voice Recognition

You can control your Smart TV, and use many of its features, with voice commands.

If you enable Voice Recognition, you can interact with your Smart TV using your voice. To provide you the Voice Recognition feature, some interactive voice commands may be trans-mitted (along with information about your device, including device identifiers) to a third-party service provider (currently, Nuance Communications, Inc.) that converts your interactive voice commands to text and to the extent necessary to provide the Voice Recognition features to you. In addition, Samsung may collect and your device may capture voice commands and associated texts so that we can provide you with Voice Recognition features and evaluate and improve the features. Samsung will collect your interactive voice commands only when you make a specific search request to the Smart TV by clicking the activation button either on the remote control or on your screen and speaking into the microphone on the remote control.

If you do not enable Voice Recognition, you will not be able to use interactive voice recognition features, although you may be able to control your TV using certain predefined voice commands.

You may disable Voice Recognition data collection at any time by visiting the "settings" menu. However, this may prevent you from using some of the Voice Recognition features.

Gesture Controls and Facial Recognition

Your SmartTV is equipped with a camera that enables certain advanced features, including the ability to control and interact with your TV with gestures and to use facial recognition technology to authenticate your Samsung Account on your TV. The camera can be covered and disabled at any time, but be aware that these advanced services will not be available if the camera is disabled.

GESTURE CONTROL. To provide you with the ability to control your SmartTV through gestures, the camera mounted on the top of your SmartTV can recognise your movements. This enables you, for example, to move between panels and zoom in or zoom out. We record information about when and how users use gesture controls so that we can evaluate the performance of these controls and improve them.

FACIAL RECOGNITION. The camera situated on the SmartTV also enables you to authenticate your Samsung Account or to log into certain services using facial recognition technology. You can use facial recognition instead of, or as a supplementary security measure in addition to, manually inputting your password.

Once you complete the steps required to set up facial recognition, an image of your face is stored locally on your TV; it is not transmitted to Samsung. If you cancel your Samsung Account or no longer desire to use facial recognition, please visit the applicable settings menu to delete the stored image. While your image will be stored locally, Samsung may take note of the fact that you have set up the feature and collect information about when and how the feature is used so that we can evaluate the performance of this feature and improve it.

Okay, so you got that?

The above is taken verbatim from a portion of the Smart TV privacy policy on Samsung's website. It is a privacy statement, and if it doesn't give you pause, then you have nerves of steel. Consider the fact that if the voice recognition feature is activated, you are being listened to all the time. It is a good illustration of the dilemma. Samsung is no doubt collecting information in large part, if not solely, to figure out how to make a better product and improve the user experience. But while they are going about improving their sales and marketing, what exactly are they doing to protect all that bizarre collateral information that might be collected in the process about your daily life—such as exactly how displeased you were that someone ate all the potato chips—not to mention all that not-so-harmless information about your viewing habits that it may or may not be collecting? And how is it to be protected? Are they spending as much on the security of your data as they are on research and development? You already know the answer.

That there is an issue with this technology is a given. It is not secure, nor was it designed to be. Simply reading Samsung's privacy statement provides a forceful reminder that products and services need to be designed and built with data security, rather than saleable novelties, in mind. It is also evidence that the captains of commerce and industry calling the shots out there have yet to truly absorb the lessons offered by the past billion or so personal information records compromised since 2005.

It is tempting to blame this on Samsung, but of course they aren't alone. You may recall the furor in 2014 over Facebook Messenger and whether its microphone access could enable snooping. The same no doubt goes for Apple's iOS 8 concierge feature, always listening to your voice (when your device is plugged in) in case you say "Hey Siri." Seems like a good project for a hacker, no? Amazon's Echo can listen in on you, too, as can Microsoft's Kinect. That said, with Samsung, a motley (or should I say mottled) crew of both white- and black-hat hackers have revealed vulnerabilities—complete with a how-to video—that are inherent in the Samsung SmartTV platform—ones that would enable, at least in theory, a cybersnoop to listen in on your conversations.

Being spied on is bad enough, but it's not the end of the story. Because this technology is used in cars, we need to think about more serious crimes, including kidnappings, extortion schemes, and murders the likes of which used to belong only in James Bond movies.

It's your third date. Romance is in the air. You've had a sumptuous dinner. You and your date are sitting on the living room couch. You put your arm around her. You pull her close to you. You begin to whisper sweet nothings in her ear. Suddenly, your iPhone, which has been charging on the coffee table, glows, and Siri loudly exclaims, "Is that the best you've got?"

Experts have warned for years that car key fob crimes were possible. In 2011, Swiss researchers announced they had cracked the encrypted remote entry systems of ten car models by eight different manufacturers, using equipment that cost as little as a hundred dollars.

Most modern cars use computers to control everything from engine compression to cruise control, airbags, and brakes. Those computers communicate with each other on open networks. Using an $80,000 grant from the Defense Advanced Research Projects Agency (DARPA), two researchers hacked the onboard computers of a Toyota Prius and a Ford Escape SUV.

They made the Prius accelerate and brake, and they jerked the wheel while the car was traveling at high speeds. They managed to turn the Ford's steering wheel at low speeds, and disable the brakes, which caused researcher Charlie Miller to drive the SUV into his garage and totally destroy his own lawnmower. Needless to say, this is a nightmare scenario, and not just for home gardeners.

"Once you are through that initial barrier, you can and will be able to do almost anything you want to," security researcher Don Bailey told NPR.

It gets worse. At an annual convention for hackers called DEF CON, Miller and his coresearcher Chris Valasek showed a large audience how they could drive a brand-new Prius remotely using a Nintendo video game controller from the 1980s. They did it by plugging a laptop into the car's on-board diagnostics

> "Want me to return control of your car now that I've caused it to accelerate to 100 MPH? Send me $10,000."

(OBD) jack, which mechanics use to diagnose mechanical problems. It is only a matter of time before this will be possible by way of a wireless hack.

If the past few years have taught us anything, it's that identity thieves, fraudsters, and scammers are on the prowl, going after any information they can use to make a buck. The other big lesson is that they think way outside the box. That's their job: to case a target and figure out how to nail it. When an architect builds a bank, he or she thinks about structural integrity, function, aesthetic considerations, and security. It's all tied together. When a thief looks at the same structure, he or she looks for vulnerabilities. The thief has the easier job. A wrecking ball doesn't need good ideas.

When it comes to IoT, the bad guys are looking at a bank that is still under construction. The walls are incomplete; we may not even agree yet on where the walls are *supposed* to be. But the money's already in there.

If the thought of being the unwitting star of your own prime-time reality show gives you the willies, consider the revelation a while back that more than 73,000 unsecured webcams and surveillance cameras were made available, viewable to all comers, on a Russian-based website. The site listed the cameras by country. The spreadsheet was impressive. The United States was well represented. In every case, victims ignored safety protocols and installed the cameras with their default login and password—admin/admin or another easy-to-guess combination findable on any number of public-facing websites.

I can tell you from basic penetration testing and other security drills on websites that I've come across in my work that the attacks are pretty much constant—most likely botnets poking around at random with programmed persistency. Where there is vulnerability, there is an algorithm that either already predicted it or will be able to find it. There are still other algorithms that can make their own weather—creating vulnerabilities where there were none.

Speaking in another context, President Kennedy's words were prescient when it comes to cybersecurity: "Things do not happen. Things are made to happen." Security doesn't happen by accident, but compromises often do.

According to Network World, reporting on the webcam story, "There are 40,746 pages of unsecured cameras just in the first 10 country listings: 11,046 in the U.S.; 6,536 in South Korea; 4,770 in China; 3,359 in Mexico; 3,285 in France; 2,870 in Italy; 2,422 in the U.K.; 2,268 in the Netherlands; 2,220 in Colombia; and 1,970 in India. Like the site said, you can see into 'bedrooms of all countries of the world.' There are 256 countries listed plus one directory not sorted into country categories."

You may remember the extortionist who hacked into the computer camera of Miss Teen USA and took compromising photographs. He tried to get money in exchange for not distributing the pictures; however, he got eighteen months behind bars instead. He also got my attention, along with the rest of the privacy and data-security community.

Unfortunately, there are thousands more where this guy came from, all of them poking around, looking for ways to exploit the private moments of your life for their personal amusement or financial gain.

While IoT can make your home smart, your fitness totally interactive, and many everyday tasks easier, the devices we buy to streamline day-to-day life create vulnerabilities that could bring your day to a screeching halt if they are ever successfully exploited. And because there are no federal regulations regarding security on IoT devices, the risks are much higher if you don't apply common sense during the setup of these password-protected products. The rule here couldn't be simpler: Anything that hooks into a network must be locked down. Be under no illusion: It won't come locked down, and it may not even tell you that it's connected. In fact, if anything, it will come in "blurt it out to the entire universe" mode. You have to assume that others have already figured out how to make you miss the pitter-pat of their digital feet in your world when you connect your IoT purchase—whether those footfalls belong to members of a marketing team, cyberthieves, or your garden-variety voyeur.

You've hopefully heard this before with regard to your Facebook account and other social media sites, but it bears repeating: Whenever you are offered something free of charge or for a negligible fee, assume that you are the product. Many companies are hoping you'll like their product and pitch it to your friends and neighbors. From the company's point of view, this form of digital pass-it-on marketing is a lot more targeted than, say, a television ad. This goes for all those products that ask you to share information about your new acquisition on social media upon registration. You are either engaged in marketing or you're helping the manufacturer or service provider to perfect whatever you just bought—or both. Regardless, you're doing something for the company that made the product—not for yourself.

In a perfect world, IoT would be . . . well, perfect. In the real world, IoT is still in the early years of its evolution, with all the lawlessness and chaos that implies. Indeed, smaller companies are rushing IoT products to market in a mad dash to beat bigger brands that have more at stake when it comes to security. As a result, you can't always be so sure that your data is going to be safe. Over the past few years, we've learned the hard way that there is no such thing as too safe or secure when it comes to cybercrime, and there is a whole host of organizations out there—both big and small—that are doing a miserable job of protecting you.

Consider the fitness wearable sold by Jawbone. It collected data about users' sleeping patterns after an earthquake in California— already uncool—and then published it. Really uncool. Frankly, whatever is worse than really uncool, that's what this was. Perhaps illegal? Alas, not yet. The data was anonymized, but as we have seen in Chapter 1, there are ways to reidentify data sets. Many users protested because they didn't realize that the product's privacy policy allowed Jawbone to do that.

A similar device called Fitbit transmitted information about users' sex lives to social media. Why? Because of the company's marketing decision to send out the product with a default setting that shared *any* information collected by the device on social media. Here are some examples: "Sexual activity. General, moderate effort. Started at 1:00 am. N/A 45 minutes." Or this: "Sexual activity. Active, vigorous effort. Started at 11:30 pm. N/A 1 hour 30 minutes." Or even the minutest detail of "Sexual activity. Passive, light effort. Kissing. hugging. N/A 10 mins."

Fitbit stopped broadcasting sexual activity after word spread of the TMI posts, and Jawbone had no issue defending their sleep trolling by saying its privacy policy was clear as day, and that the company didn't share individual data without consent. Both in-

Time for a Privacy Disclosure Box?

I've written at length about the need for federal legislation that provides umbrella protections of privacy and data for consumers (Chapter 14 details a few proposals), but here is an area screaming for a regulation.

One model that might work is something along the lines of the Schumer box, which is a summary mandated by law of the costs of a credit card in the United States. Under this law, credit card companies are required to list long-term rates in at least 18-point type and other key disclosures in 12-point type, including annual fee (if applicable), annual percentage rate for purchases (APR), transaction fees, and so on.

A privacy disclosure box might include

- what information the company sells to third parties;
- disclosures about tracking your Internet use;
- whether the device is able to record or snoop via camera or microphone;
- how data collected from the device is used; and
- how data collected from the device is stored.

Whether this could be part of a larger privacy and data-security bill is a question for lawmakers to answer.

formation gushers were enabled by untoward privacy policies—unread by early adopters—and users' false assumptions that these products came with privacy controls set tightly as a default, if they thought about privacy settings at all.

Don't think your IoT device will cause you any problems? Consider this: There are destinations online—not even on the dark web, just right there for public consumption—that list the default passwords of every kind of IoT device on the market today. Because there is no regulation governing how these devices come into your possession, if you have something wireless that's hooking

---

There Oughta Be a Law

I know what you're thinking: We should tell Washington to fix this, demand regulations that protect unwitting consumers from the overreaches of corporate marketing departments. But I think it's a mistake to think this way. Seriously, why waste the ink here? We all know that's not going to happen any time soon. Meanwhile, there's the problem, leaking personal information like a newspaper.

Here's the truth: You have to protect yourself. The assumption that there is an honor system whereby your private information will be protected by third parties is a pipe dream. You are the ultimate guardian of your information. You're the one who will get hosed if it gets out there, so you are the one who should make sure that it doesn't.

Assume that you need to set your own long and strong password, and that every shred of your personal information is being passed along to third (and fourth and fifth) parties, and then do the following:

- Share only what you'd want to have the world know about you.
- Set your permissions accordingly.

---

up to your household router, it very likely came with a preset password and login. And there's a good chance that, whatever the device, there's a forum online where it's been figured out, hacked, cracked, and hijacked for all stripes of nefarious purposes.

The added convenience provided by the IoT is obvious, but the security issues may not be. Are your fitness records hackable by a third party? Are they linked to social media? How much information is required to access them? A login? A password? And what's to stop a hacker from locking or unlocking your front door, disabling your alarm system, or turning off your heat during a blizzard or your lights during a home invasion—all with an app? The answer is, not very much.

Other common devices that are password protected should immediately come to mind here. Whether it is your household printer, your wireless router, or your DVR, there are folks out there who are very curious about you, not because they value you as a human being, but because they can create value from any plugged-in human—whether by fraud or extortion or (in a more old-fashioned mode) getting the information they need to rob you blind when you're not home. And even if they don't want to know about you, they may want to enlist your devices in a spam distribution effort.

The number of people who don't change default passwords is staggering, as evidenced by the 73,000 wide-open webcams on that Russian website. There's a major disconnect here, and it's specific to the IoT. On the Internet proper, it seems the message has finally sunk in and people are beginning to make themselves harder targets—making sure their privacy settings are tight and their passwords are both strong and changed frequently. But when it comes the IoT, there is still more learning to be done—hopefully not the hard way.

The solution for this particular problem is remarkably simple: Set a long and strong password on all devices. Whatever it is, it's your job to pick something easy for you to remember and hard for others to guess. The industry standard here that would save everyone a lot of self-reliance would of course be an agreed-upon system designed as a protocol for any networkable device: namely, that they cannot be activated without a long and strong, multi-symbol password.

I keep coming back to a Pew Research Center statistic on the public perception of privacy and personal information released in early 2014 that stated that 91 percent of Americans felt they had lost control of their personal information, because it says so much about where we are right now. If over 90 percent of Americans believe they have no control over their personal information—that the facts and figures and ciphers unique to them are simply in too many places, and essentially that the data cat's out of the bag, what incentive do they have to protect their sensitive data? Clearly, not much. That said, if businesses were to start behaving like they cared about protecting data, and respecting the privacy of their customers, it seems pretty reasonable to suspect that the many Americans who feel completely lost on the information frontier might start to feel like they had some control over their data.

It could be a while before business practices change. My advice, in the meantime, is to change your own.

7

A Taxing Situation

IRS commissioner John A. Koskinen sent out an email on January 14, 2015, that maybe shouldn't have been in the news. But, somehow, it found its way into the media. Writing about budget cuts, funding shortfalls, and what it would all mean for consumers, Koskinen didn't mince words, though I would argue that his purportedly frank subject line, "Budget update: Tough choices," could have been more simply put as, "We're Screwed."

In the leaked email, the commissioner detailed the funding situation: "Congress approved a $10.9 billion budget for us, which means we must absorb a cut of $346 million during the remaining nine months of the fiscal year. But that really amounts to a total reduction of about $600 million when you count another $250 million in mandated costs and inflation."

Later in the email, Koskinen explained why the cuts would hurt: "new taxpayer protections against identity theft will be delayed."

"We have no choice but to do less with less," Koskinen wrote.

What exactly does "less" look like? As far as our purposes in this book go, it looks like more tax-related identity theft. There was an 83 percent reduction in the agency's budget for training employees—training that presumably these days revolves to a large extent around ways to reduce tax-related fraud. Additionally, the contracting cash pool at the IRS has meant 12,000 fewer employees at the agency at a time when, if anything, the increases in tax-related fraud should result in a hiring frenzy.

The budget cuts inflicted on the Internal Revenue Service mean fewer people to answer phones, check records, and perform audits. In fact, the agency came right out and said (in a real press release, not just a leaked memo) that they won't be able to respond to 57 percent of calls received during tax season, written correspondence will go unanswered for months, and callers will have to wait on average for thirty minutes before they get a human on the line. And once you do get someone from the IRS on the phone, don't expect too much. They will only answer basic tax-law questions—and then only during tax-filing season. If you're late, you're on your own.

Meanwhile, the Treasury estimates that the IRS could issue $21 billion to identity thieves over the next five years. If this number is too large to contemplate, consider that $21 billion could pay for any of the below big-ticket items, if it weren't being sent by the government directly to thieves:

- An entire year's worth of funding for NASA, with $2 billion to spare
- Three years' worth of maintenance for our nuclear stockpile, or ten years of fighting nuclear proliferation around the world
- Twenty years' worth of loan guarantees for efficient, renewable energy projects
- More than twenty years' worth of funding for the Federal Highway Administration
- Almost five years' worth of funding for the Food and Drug Administration
- Five and a half years' worth of Homeland Security disaster preparedness grants to states and local communities

Tax-Related Scams

Phone

If you get a phone call from the IRS, hang up. It doesn't matter what your caller ID says. Spoofing a number is not a terribly difficult project for someone working an IRS phone scam. The actual form this scam takes depends on the person running it. The caller might give you a badge number. He or she might even have your Social Security number, or the last four digits of it.

The caller may threaten you with jail time. They may know details about you. It may seem real. But again, if you get a call like this, hang up and dial the IRS at 800-829-1040. Bear in mind that recent budget cuts mean you will probably be in a caller queue for the better part of an hour, only to be told there is no one who can talk to you about your issue.

Or just bear this in mind: The IRS will never initiate contact by phone. If they do, believe me, it's not them—it's a scam.

Phishing

Do you know what's even more unlikely than the IRS calling to threaten you with jail time when they don't even have enough staff to properly vet incoming tax returns for signs of tax fraud? I'll save you a guess: getting an email from the IRS.

The IRS only contacts taxpayers via the U.S. Postal Service. While it may feel strange and transgressive, should an email from the IRS arrive in your inbox, don't reply. Trash it. And do the same with any other request for your information that comes by way of email—even if it's legitimate. Many companies and organizations have terrible data hygiene practices. Get on the phone and provide what's asked for (assuming you make the call and are in control of the conversation).

Crooked Accountants and Other Miscreants

If someone promises you a ginormous tax refund—bigger than anything your accountant could get you—run.

This particular variety of bottom-feeding fraudster—a fake accountant, essentially—subsists on a steady diet of elderly clients and low-income filers. A few hallmarks of phony filers include: asking you to sign an incomplete tax return; refusing to sign the tax return themselves; or refusing to provide you with a copy of the return filed in their name. Another common strategy is directing the refund to the fraudulent filer's bank account. From there, the scammer either skims a huge fee (also known as stealing money) or they just keep the entire refund.

You Are Who You Hire

It can be great to hire someone to prepare your taxes (as 60 percent of taxpayers do). It takes a lot of the guesswork out of the equation. That is, of course, unless the "professional" you hire is engaging in guesswork. Are you sure the person preparing your taxes is an accountant or at least works with one they can consult? When it comes to choosing a tax preparer, there should be zero guesswork. Hire someone you've thoroughly checked out, and who has three solid references—at least one of them coming from someone you trust.

Why? Well, whatever they do, you do. Your signature goes on the return, and if there are fraudulent items in it, you're the one who could wind up in prison.

Was That the Salvation Army or Salvation Arnie?

Fake charities are something you should always be worried about, but especially beware of using any tax deduction you're not 100 percent sure about.

Contributing to tax-deductible charities is a great way to reduce your taxes, but you have to make sure they are legit. When making a donation, ask them to provide appropriate documentation that is acceptable to the IRS. If you are not sure the charity is for real, it's a good idea to ask them for the letter of determination from the IRS regarding their 501(c) status.

The budget shortfall at the IRS could hardly have come at a worse time. From April 2011 through the fourth quarter of 2014, the IRS stopped 19 million suspicious tax returns and protected more than $63 billion in fraudulent refunds. While that's probably heroic on some level, we should ask: Heroic compared to what? Identity thieves filing fraudulent returns during the 2013 tax-filing season drained the Treasury Department of $5.8 billion. That the IRS was able to prevent the loss of another $24.2 billion during the same time period is bittersweet news. Who knows how much of that $5.8 billion could have been saved if not for the budget cuts?

True to Koskinen's word (or what could be divined from his leaked email), 2015 was a dicey year for anything tax related. Perhaps most noteworthy, as mentioned in Chapter 3, the software giant Intuit temporarily suspended the electronic filing of all state tax returns following a marked uptick in what appeared to be fraudulent filings. The escalation of those filings at the state level may have something to do with inroads that the IRS made in protecting itself from the onslaught of fraudulent returns over the past three years—a system of protocols and triggers that, for good reason, we know very little about. Whether the IRS is matching salary information to previous tax returns filed by a consumer, or some other method of augury to distinguish the true from the false in tax filings, the shift on the part of identity thieves to state returns probably suggests the feds have been doing a better than abysmal job.

With major data breaches like those at Anthem and Premera that between them exposed 91 million Social Security numbers, identity thieves have gained access to all the personally identifiable information they need to commit tax identity theft for several years to come. We have every reason to believe the problem will continue to plague the IRS. After all, it was only in 2012 that the IRS initiated the Law Enforcement Assistance Program (LEAP), which was designed to get a handle on tax refund fraud—or at least part of it. The program was supposed to aid taxpayers and help law enforcement with all stripes of tax-related identity theft. The program started in Florida, a hotbed of identity-related fraud and scams, in April 2012, and six months later it left its cocoon in the Sunshine State to become a federal program.

LEAP provided law enforcement with Form 8821-A, IRS Disclosure Authorization for Victims of Identity Theft. The basic point of this bureaucratic widget was to enable law enforcement officers to request a victim's tax information from the IRS in the hope that something in the return might lead back to the responsible party. After the program's rollout, there was a U.S. Treasury Inspector General for Tax Administration (TIGTA) audit, to see how efficiently the IRS was processing the new requests from law enforcement. After looking at a sample pulled from the total filed between January 3 and September 27, 2013—2,481 to be exact—TIGTA grabbed about two hundred.

The audit revealed that thirty-nine requests had been rejected, but eight—or 20 percent—of those requests should have been approved. Another eleven "were invalid or incomplete and should not have been processed due to the risk of unauthorized disclosure." (They were released anyway, opening the door to possible identity theft.) Speed was another problem. More than half of the requests took more than ten days to complete. Perhaps most worrisome of all, the IRS couldn't tell TIGTA what information had been furnished to law enforcement in 72 percent of the sample cases because they didn't keep records.

If the government's anti–identity theft laws are opening the door for more identity theft, you know we have a problem.

Tax refund fraud losses are estimated to reach $21 billion by 2016, according to the Treasury Inspector General for Tax Administration, which provides independent oversight of the IRS.

While the massive loss chronicled in the January 2015 United States Government Accountability Report was big news (for a nanosecond anyway), the GAO's recommendations for stemming

When I asked Senators Elizabeth Warren and Gary Peters what they would do with the $5.8 billion that the IRS has sent to fraudsters, here's what they said.

Sen. Elizabeth Warren, D-MA

"$5.8 billion could have increased the National Institutes of Health budget for the year by more than 15 percent. Right now, NIH can fund only one in six research proposals, and many young researchers are getting discouraged and leaving the field. Think how many young researchers could have had their careers launched with that $5.8 billion—and think about the break-throughs on Alzheimer's or autism or diabetes that they might have made."

Sen. Gary C. Peters, D-MI

"Cracking down on identity theft and false tax returns would not only save American families from financial hardship and frustra-tion, it would free up funds to reinvest in our nation's future. I would divide the $5.8 billion in savings between the Head Start Program and basic science research at the National Science Foundation. The Head Start Program is one of the most success-ful federal programs we have. Providing critical education, health, nutrition, and social services to low-income families helps ensure that all American children have a chance to succeed in school, regardless of their ZIP code. The National Science Foundation funds all fields of fundamental science, research, and engineering—the seeds that will grow our future economy. Investing in scientific research is critical to increasing America's competitiveness, driving innovation, and creating new jobs."

the rising tide of tax-related fraud did not get a lot of attention, which was remarkable after the leaked email from Commissioner Koskinen's office. With funding cuts at the IRS, it's a certainty that the 2015 tax season will make headlines for record-breaking re-fund fraud.

The GAO report made many things clear to me, but one point stands out: The only way to stop tax refund fraud is to change the way the tax filing and refund system works, and while this may be a painful process for employers and taxpayers alike, it's necessary.

In 2012, the IRS received more than 148 million tax returns. The agency issued almost $310 billion in refunds to approximately 110.5 million taxpayers. That is a lot to keep track of, a fact that is not lost on identity thieves. According to the GAO report, by March 1, 2012—a month and a half before the filing deadline—the IRS had already paid out around half of that year's tax refunds. If that timing sounds odd to you, well, it's a big part of the problem.

When the fiscal year ends and you begin the less than pleasant process of preparing your taxes, employers also get to work on filing your W-2 with the government. The feds then compare your tax return to the W-2 your employer files to make sure everything matches up. But here's the catch: Employers don't have to file W-2 wage data until March 2, if they file on paper, and March 31 for e-filers. So, half of the refunds in 2012 were sent out on blind faith. As things stand now, the IRS only starts the process of matching employer-reported W-2 data to tax returns in July, long after most refunds have been issued. It's called "look-back" compliance.

Does that sound crazy to you? Well, it is. Part of the reason for the slow compliance check is that W-2s have to go through the Social Security Administration before being sent over to the IRS. Why it's done this way is anyone's guess, but it doesn't matter. Until it is changed, tax refund fraud is only going to get worse.

That said, a simple (and necessary) change applied to the flow of information is not going to solve the problem by itself. The IRS uses look-back compliance for an important reason: to get money back to taxpayers as soon as possible. Many taxpayers rely on refunds to make ends meet, and as a result the IRS is under enormous congressional pressure to issue refunds promptly. In fact, the agency is required by law to pay interest if it takes longer than forty-five days after the tax return's due date (typically April 15) to issue a refund.

It is by dint of this system that most taxpayers can expect a refund within twenty-one days of filing their tax return.

The refund process as it stands now makes sense only as the quaint relic of simpler times. It's the epitome of an analog approach getting trounced by our digital reality. Not to put too fine a point on it, but I believe look-back compliance should go the way of the horse and buggy.

There is no simple solution that can make this happen overnight. The GAO's suggestion of earlier W-2 filing deadlines might allow the IRS to match employer-reported wage information to taxpayers' returns before issuing refunds. The recommendation in the report was to move up the employers' deadline from March 31 to January 31. This could be facilitated by requiring all employers to e-file W-2s, instead of the current arrangement, which states that only companies with more than 250 employees have to e-file. Paper filing costs more, and it takes longer, which exacerbates the problem. It was probably time to institute mandatory W-2 e-filing a decade ago, but better late than never.

The other solution, unfortunately, may involve changing the rules about refunds—or possibly even pushing tax day to later in the year. The GAO also brought up the possibility of delaying refunds, which is probably the most controversial recommendation from the taxpayers' viewpoint. After all, many Americans use their refunds to pay down debt, buy a new car, or just help them pay their bills on time. A longer wait for a refund would clearly be unpopular, but the current situation is actually costing taxpayers more.

Tax refunds must be verified in order to keep them from landing in the wrong hands. The way to make this happen is by ending look-back compliance, or with a drastic systems improvement.

I am not discounting the trouble the above suggestions could cause for people. Loans to bridge the time people spend waiting for refund checks wastes money that would be better spent on the necessities of life. But the tax fraud problem is rapidly becoming an epidemic, and it may require significant adjustments to the ways wages are reported and refunds are issued. This process is unpleasant, but it may be quite necessary.

The IRS has tried a few reactive measures that have only had limited success, but I don't think that means they should stop trying. For instance, the IRS may want to take their lead from amusement parks, many of which are using biometrics—specifically fingerprint readers. The technology is now cheap enough for the federal government to require that all tax preparers have a biometric fingerprint reader wherever they do business. If you were to prepare your own taxes and e-file, you would likely need a biometric device at home. (They can be had for around $100.) Congress could give a $100 tax credit to home e-filers who purchase a biometric device to authenticate their electronically filed tax return. Chances are good that the tax break would pay for itself, as tax refunds would be sent to consumers instead of wasted on scammers.

If this sounds too extreme, how about transaction notifications? Banks and credit card companies offer it already. In the simplest of terms, it would work the same way with IRS transactions. Every time something involving your Social Security number happens at the IRS, you receive a letter in the mail letting you know about it. When the letter is triggered, all work on the return stops till the taxpayer confirms—either by phone or by mail, whichever the security pros determine to be safer—that they filed the return. Since this could get costly, it might be that the IRS charges for the service. With regard to tax fraud, identity thieves would stop trying because it would no longer be easy.

What to Do If You Are a Victim of Tax Identity Theft

REPORT THE CRIME. File a report with your local police and file a complaint with the Federal Trade Commission at www .identitytheft.gov or by calling the FTC Identity Theft Hotline at 1-877-438-4338.

REQUEST A FRAUD ALERT. Contact one of the three major credit reporting agencies, Equifax, Experian, or TransUnion, and ask that a fraud alert be placed on your credit records.

CONSIDER ENROLLING IN CREDIT MONITORING PROGRAMS. You might wish to purchase a combination credit and fraud monitoring service, which provides instant alerts whenever anyone attempts to open a credit account in your name. This can be an effective backup to fraud alerts.

CLOSE FRAUDULENT ACCOUNTS. Close any credit or financial account that has been tampered with by a thief or opened without your permission.

CONTACT THE IRS. Call the number provided on the IRS notice informing you of the fraud. To clear your tax record, complete IRS Form 14039, Identity Theft Affidavit. You can use a fillable form at www.IRS.gov, print it, then mail or fax it.

PAY YOUR TAXES. Be sure to continue to pay your taxes and file your tax returns on time, even if you must do so by mailing in paper forms.

STAY DILIGENT. If you contacted the IRS about taxpayer ID theft and did not receive a resolution, contact the Identity Protection Specialized Unit at 1-800-908-4490 about your case.

STAY ALERT. You have to assume that if someone has enough of your personal information to file a tax return, they have more than enough information to commit other forms of identity theft. Read every explanation of benefits statement and be sensitive to any communication you may receive from a debt collector. It may not be a mistake.

8

It's a Hard-Knock Life

Child Identity Theft

Every two seconds. That was the pace at which Americans became victims of identity theft in 2013—and that's just the cases we know about.

Identity theft is the fastest-growing crime in this country, and is spreading like a cancer throughout the world. There are new methods born every day. In fact, statistics from 2013 aren't very helpful, because it's worse now. I wouldn't be surprised if we see multiple people getting got every second before the epidemic hits its apogee.

Then there are all the unreported cases, where shame trumps the desire for justice. Many cases never get reported either because the victim just wants to get on with his or her life or because they are too embarrassed to talk about being scammed. The shame factor is particularly strong when an identity-related crime is committed by a close friend or family member.

Somewhere between 10 and 16 million Americans get got every year by the various scams and frauds that are already out there, and with the ways and means to perpetrate identity-related crimes ever on the rise, those numbers will continue to increase.

The more startling identity theft statistic that doesn't get nearly enough play is the number of people who are victimized by those closest to them.

Family members account for more than 30 percent of the identity-related fraudsters who get caught. Another 18 percent of the fraudsters committing identity theft were friends. That's nearly half of all reported identity-related crimes.

Identity theft is a crime of opportunity. The easier it is to take advantage of you, the more likely it is that you will become a victim. That's one of the rules of the identity theft jungle. And that's the reason identity thieves so often do double duty as family members or people within a family's circle of trust. No one has a greater opportunity to exploit you than a family member.

Axton Betz-Hamilton knows this only too well.

Born in Indiana, she was raised in a solidly middle-class home. Her mother Pamela was a tax preparer and her dad worked as the department manager for a grocery store. There was nothing extraordinary about her childhood. But by the time she was in college, things were starting to get a little weird. She had become the victim of identity theft. She didn't have to look far to find the culprit.

Betz-Hamilton's particular identity theft story is not only a family affair—it's a journey in dysfunction far stranger than fiction.

"We lived on hobby farms—one in Portland, Indiana, and then another in Redkey," Betz-Hamilton told me. She spent Thanksgivings with her family, and they went the way most do, as did Christmases. Her family was by no means wealthy, so when her paternal grandfather couldn't make it on his own, he moved in with Betz-Hamilton's mom and dad. That was in the 1990s. Her grandfather had been a welder at a tractor factory. Together, they were a small family unit that looked like many others in middle-class America. In reality, they were ensnared in a mindboggling circle of financial fraud that revolved around one family member who was fleecing the other three.

"Nineteen Thanksgivings came and went, and my mother cooked those dinners for us—me and Dad and my grandfather after he moved in in 1995. We were getting robbed by the hand that fed us the entire time," she told me when I called to hear her story.

The story of Betz-Hamilton's journey into the hell of identity theft spans twenty years. It started in 1993, but she's still dealing with the fallout even today. That's the reality. It's a crime that leaves marks, and it doesn't have to be a massive hit. The charges on credit cards that were acquired using her Social Security number amounted to about $4,000—a little lower than the average take of $4,841—but the damage was like a bad water leak in the upper floors of a house—unpredictable and pervasive.

She found out the way most people do—while going about her life. Betz-Hamilton had no idea that she had been victimized until she was a nineteen-year-old college student and wanted to move off campus. She found an apartment with little ado, but the utility company didn't want to give her an account without a deposit. They asked for $100. The reason was mindboggling: She had very bad credit.

So she did what anyone should do in the same situation. She ordered a copy of her credit report to see what was going on. She was expecting a letter-sized envelope containing a page or two of transactions. What she got was a thick manila envelope, heavy with bad news.

"My credit report was ten pages long, and my credit score was 380," Betz-Hamilton told me.

Her credit report chronicled a completely fictional financial past. Confused and worried that she might not be able to get it cleared up right away, she contacted the Identity Theft Resource Center, a nonprofit organization dedicated to helping victims of identity theft. They told her to file a police report. She did that, and waited as nothing happened.

Getting your affairs sorted out after a deeply entrenched pattern of fraud is very difficult, as Betz-Hamilton discovered. The police are often of little use, because even if they get involved—and they often will just suggest you take up the matter with the companies where the fraud happened—the cases are very difficult to investigate and they present a myriad of problems regarding jurisdiction and evidence.

It gets even worse if the person who defrauded you is smart. When Betz-Hamilton tried to dispute the accounts with one of the credit card companies where her fraudster mom had an account, she was informed that they weren't going to take action. Her story did not hold up, because her mom had been clever: She had made two payments before maxing out the account. This was earlier in the evolution of identity theft, so the credit card company in question can be forgiven for not recognizing this as a fraudster's trick, but it is not uncommon for an identity thief to try to extend the value of a target by strategically paying a couple of bills in the beginning to make things appear as normal as possible.

The consequences Betz-Hamilton faced will be familiar to anyone who has ever struggled with a bad credit history. She had to pay higher interest rates for her car loan as well as for the credit cards she had obtained herself. Her first car loan rate was a whopping 18.23 percent, and her first credit card had a 29.9 percent annual percentage rate. For a long time, she had to pay deposits for electric, phone, and cable services. And until 2009, she paid higher insurance rates. All this goes to show that there are hidden costs absorbed by victims of identity theft. Indeed, the lifetime costs of identity theft are staggering, since bad credit can impact so many pieces of your financial life.

So how did it start?

Betz-Hamilton's parents had been victims of identity theft in 1993. It sure seemed like the real deal, not something perpetrated by her mom to look like an outside fraudster. So, after Betz-Hamilton discovered that her identity had been stolen, it seemed reasonable to think that whoever had stolen her parents' identities had stolen hers as well. It took twenty years and a fluke discovery for her to learn the truth.

Pamela Betz died of cancer in 2013, and that's when the details of her secret life started to drop from the family tree like so many rotten apples. Mama Betz had stolen her daughter's identity. She had stolen her husband's identity, too. She had even compromised her father-in-law for around $1,500. And, of course, she herself had mountains of debt.

The scary part is that the thief was right there living with the victims, and they had no idea. Traces of her crimes were squirreled away all over the property in outbuildings, books, and other hiding places. Betz-Hamilton's father made the initial discovery when he opened a blue plastic file box in one of the outbuildings on their farm. Inside, there was a twelve-year-old credit card statement. The account was in his daughter Axton's name. It was overdue, so he called his daughter to give her a hard time about this hidden bit of past ignominy. Her answer to his teasing shocked him. She told him that the card never existed. After a little back and forth, he took a closer look at the bills. Upon closer inspection, he noticed the account had a card in his wife's name.

"She had a lot of purses and backpacks, and that's where she stored the paper trail," Betz-Hamilton recalled. "It was also between dresser drawers. Papers were folded and shoved into books. We didn't know my grandfather's identity had been stolen until I found a credit card statement in one of those purses, and I still don't know how far back that goes."

Questions arose. Was there another house somewhere, cars, or perhaps another life? As Betz-Hamilton's mother lay on her deathbed, her father had become alarmed that his wife's wedding ring was missing but that detail only made sense after Mrs. Betz's crimes came to light.

"We think she pawned it," Betz-Hamilton told me. "I have no idea what she was up to. Maybe she had a second life. She had been using multiple names. I'm still looking."

Dr. Axton Betz-Hamilton is now a professor at Eastern Illinois University, where she teaches courses on personal finance and consumer issues. She wrote her doctoral dissertation on how people experience child identity theft, looking specifically at victims under the age of eighteen who learn about their situation later in life.

"My mother's last wishes were to be cremated, and we respected that. She wanted her ashes to be with me. I'm sitting next to my mother right now," she told me when I spoke to her on the phone.

"Sometimes I yell at her. And sometimes I shake the box she's in. We just don't know who mom was. It's hard to grieve for her. To change things up and start new traditions, I had Christmas at my house last year. Mom was here on the shelf. It was awkward."

The stories of child-related identity theft—like that of Axton Betz-Hamilton—are legion, each sadder and more tragic than the last. Nowhere is that tragedy more in evidence than in the foster-care community, where children are often moved through several group homes before they age out of the program. At each new way station, their personal identifying information—reduced to a data card—is passed from family to family or supervisor to supervisor like so many credit card applications in waiting. Many look at the foster child as nothing more than a meal ticket, but some see the child as a meal ticket brimming with further economic promise—not for the child, but for the thief.

It is estimated that more than 10 percent of all foster children are victims of identity theft. There is a provision to the Child and Family Services Improvement and Innovation Act introduced by Rep. Jim Langevin (D-RI) that requires that a credit check be done before a child ages out of the system. If anything seems amiss, that record must be cleaned up before he or she goes out in the world. But oftentimes, because of this experience, a victim of child identity theft is slightly more damaged than those who have not suffered the humiliation of this piling on.

So why are children such a delicious target for identity thieves? It's called runway. A child's Social Security number is pristine. There is no reason for a minor to use it in connection with any financial or credit-related transaction before reaching the age of eighteen—when he or she then becomes legally responsible for any contract they sign. Consequently, there's been no need for them, or their parents, to check their credit. That, unfortunately, has changed.

A pristine Social Security number in the hands of a skilled identity thief can be a ticket to truckloads of credit and significant cash. It holds the promise of an undisturbed romp for fifteen years or more. Just think of all the bank accounts that could be opened; all the credit cards, personal loans, student loans, car loans, and mortgages that could be secured; all the apartments that could be rented; all the smartphones, utilities, and cable and Internet services that could be obtained; all the medical treatments, prescriptions, and devices that could be purchased; all the tax refunds that could be mined; all the illegal jobs that could be obtained; and all the welfare or unemployment benefits that could be had with a gaggle of unblemished, unmonitored Social Security numbers and more than a decade of wide-open road?

Depending on the study, it is estimated that somewhere between 140,000 and 400,000 children become victims of identity theft every year. That truly is an estimate, because most children who become victims have no clue that they are being shamelessly exploited for a significant portion of their young lives; when they finally discover they have been violated, they learn very quickly that there is no magic switch to make the pain go away. In fact, they are guilty until proven innocent.

Many have absolutely no idea how it happened, and it takes time to track this down and document everything. And while the situation is being investigated and (maybe) resolved, their credit has been decimated and their ability to participate in the economy is limited. Countless victims can't get a loan, find someone to rent them an apartment, get a utility or cell phone turned on without a hefty deposit, open their mailbox without receiving some letter referencing a creditor they've never heard of, or get or keep a job in an already difficult job market, and they even, on occasion, get arrested for a crime they didn't commit in a state where they have neither lived nor visited.

Often a parent (or guardian) is the first line of defense when the whisper of a problem surfaces: an unexplained call from a debt collector, a preapproved credit card offer in their child's name, a blocked federal or state tax return due to a previous filing in the same tax year using their child's Social Security number, an application for their child's first driver's license denied due to accumulated tickets or reckless driving charges in another state (or because a valid driver's license already exists in their name). Unfortunately, many parents miss these early warning signals.

When a child learns of the crime and then discovers, as Axton Betz-Hamilton did, that the perpetrator was her mother, it is both economically challenging and emotionally dislocating. As has been reported in a number of annual ITRC "Aftermath" surveys, the spillover effects for identity theft victims go far beyond dollars and cents. There is a sense of violation, a loss of trust, and a loss of self-respect. It is indeed a hard knock to a young person's life.

So what can we do about this?

To evaluate solutions, it is instructive to go back to the root of the problem. According to a *Huffington Post* article by Gerry Smith, for decades there was no reason for children to have Social Security numbers. Then, some thirty years ago, the US government mandated that if parents wanted to claim their children as dependents on their tax returns, they had to list their children's

Cameron Noble, Child Identity Theft Victim

The run-around was exquisite. That is, exquisitely painful. When Cameron Noble first tried to resolve his identity theft problem, he was told that there had been no crime just an error. There had been no malfeasance. Noble was merely the victim of a keystroke error.

So how did he know a crime had happened? The twenty-two-year-old Utah resident started receiving notices that his wages were being garnished for back payments on child support in California.

When Cameron was seven, his parents got the first inkling that something was amiss after receiving a notice from the IRS that their son was too old to qualify as a dependent on their joint tax return. After disputing the matter, they were told their son was a middle-aged, deadbeat dad named Jose Zavala who lived two states over in California. After some back and forth, the Nobles thought they had put the matter to rest. They had not, as was evidenced fifteen years later when then the wage garnishment began.

When he tried to resolve the matter, Noble's credit reports all came to his address, but with Jose Zavala's name. In 2007, his tax refund was withheld to pay for Zavala's child support, and in 2008 he got a notice that he owed back taxes.

Understandably, he asked the Social Security Administration to issue him a new Social Security number, but they refused because they believed the explanation was, indeed, a keystroke error. After Noble enlisted help from resolution experts, the Social Security Administration finally agreed that his was a case of identity theft.

Social Security numbers in those filings. So, in order to take advantage of this deduction, parents rushed to secure a Social Security number for their children, particularly newborns. We know what happened next. Countless organizations began asking (in some cases requiring) parents to provide their child's Social Security number in connection with a variety of activities. Then those organizations got breached.

When credit reports are pulled, credit bureaus match the name, the birth date, and the Social Security number, but their only point of reference for the age of the applicant is the date of birth on the first credit application filed by that particular applicant. Crawling through that data crack, identity thieves simply combine a child's stolen Social Security number with the name and birthday of another person, creating the appearance of a new borrower (think immigrant or college graduate), and voila! They have just birthed a new, pristine credit profile.

Many argue that the Social Security Administration could solve the problem by simply permitting companies to validate that a particular Social Security number belongs to a child. Since 2008, the SSA has implemented a process that allows companies to do precisely this—if they fork over a $5,000 set-up fee, plus $1 for every check the company asks the SSA to perform. This has made it prohibitively expensive for many companies because, according to the article, they don't believe it is their responsibility to help. I remain mystified as to why no one is raising this issue in Congress. Doubtless the SSA needs to get every penny it can, but by not making this information more readily available at a reasonable price, is the government not cutting off its nose to spite its face? Making the information cheaply available would appear to be a sensible fix for a very serious issue that is draining billions of dollars from the economy and the Treasury every year. This is a prime example of how government and business should be working together but simply aren't.

That said, there is another alternative if we can't get the SSA to see the light: The 17-10 Registry. This proposal was floated by the Identity Theft Resource Center a few years ago. While it requires some refinement, it represents a meaningful solution.

Based on the model of the Social Security Death Index, the 17-10 Registry would contain certain personal identifying information on every child under the age of eighteen—when many young people begin looking to buy a car, apply for a student loan, and/or obtain their first credit card. However, since the enactment of the Credit Card Accountability, Responsibility, and Disclosure Act, young people under the age of twenty-one have more limited opportunities to acquire credit cards.

From the moment a child receives a Social Security number, until they reach the age of seventeen years and ten months, their name, month and year of birth, and Social Security number would be indexed here. Every time someone applies for credit or employment, their application will be run against the 17-10 database. If there is a match, credit extenders and employers will be required to investigate further before approving a loan or making the hire. The sheer existence of this registry would represent a powerful deterrent to identity thieves because it effectively addresses the inability of credit issuers and others to match the Social Security numbers of minors with names and birth dates.

Some states, like Utah, are experimenting with a slightly different version of this concept. They are cross-referencing an employment database with a list of children receiving public assistance in an effort to identify those using children's Social Security numbers to secure employment.

There has been no national rush to adopt this concept because many privacy advocates have raised serious concerns about the dangers of having such an omnibus compilation of information about children in one database. Imagine, they say, if it were constantly accessed by the NSA—is anything not?—or hacked.

Another alternative might entail the development and implementation of a unique identification system by which minors would be issued an eight- or ten-digit number that would be changed on their eighteenth birthday to the traditional nine-digit number. Yet, in a way, this proposal misses the point; perhaps we should be kicking our addiction to Social Security numbers in the first place.

Until that happens, though, let me provide some tips for parents who are concerned about the safety of their children's PII.

In most cases, your child shouldn't have a credit report until credit has been granted in his or her name. If you get an unexplained call or collection letter, preapproved credit card offer, IRS notice, insurance bill, explanation of benefits regarding a mystery visit to a pediatrician or nonexistent medical procedure, do not simply blow it off as a mistake. Contact the three national credit reporting agencies (Experian, Equifax, and TransUnion) and be prepared to verify your child's identity as well as your authority as parent or guardian.

They require you to document your child's name, address, and date of birth, as well as to provide copies of his or her birth certificate and Social Security card. They'll need copies of your driver's license (or similar proof of your identity with the same address) and a utility bill showing that your address is current.

While each bureau may have slightly different questions, the process is the same for the most part. There are also services offered by the bureaus and several third-party resellers that monitor your child's credit and identity. It is worth taking the time to do your research to find the best program for you.

If all goes well, all of this will be for naught—literally. If there is no credit report, your child's financial future awaits them in the form of a blank slate. But if you do discover that they have a credit file containing accounts—the result of an identity theft—you must work with the fraud departments of the credit bureaus (as well as notify the police, the creditors, and the government as appropriate) to eliminate the fraudulent accounts and then suppress your child's credit profile until they turn eighteen. It is one of the greatest gifts you will ever give them.

The main takeaway here is that, as parents, we have a fiduciary duty to protect our children. One important way to stand up for them and help them build the right foundation for an economically secure future is to keep a watchful eye on their PII and to move swiftly in the event there is the slightest hint that their information has been compromised.

9

May the Farce Be with You

Social Media Dos and Don'ts

Social media is a huge part of daily life for many people; some even find it hard to imagine living without it. We use it to check in with friends, keep tabs on family members, shop for jobs and new purchases, and stay abreast of the latest breaking news. And let's not forget the flame wars in product reviews and comment sections. No matter your preferred means of self-expression, social media drastically expands your attackable surface for hackers.

If you want to minimize your exposure to the threat of identity theft, it is imperative that you become master of your domain—at least as it exists on other domains like Facebook, Twitter, Tumblr, Pinterest, Instagram, and LinkedIn. And by "master" I mean that you need to learn how to use it in a way that minimizes your exposure to the threat of identity theft.

> You don't have to stop using social media, but you probably do need to consider changing the way you use it.

The Pew Research Center's statistics for social media in 2014 showed that 74 percent of Americans used some form of social media, and more than 71 percent of these users have a presence on Facebook.

While I'm going to talk about Facebook here, feel free to pick your poison, because when it comes to social media, there isn't a company out there that doesn't make you an easier target for identity thieves. As far as the Three Ms go, the same thinking applies regardless of the venue. If you're going to use social media, you must take steps to minimize your exposure.

Some people like the puppy pics and game app requests of Facebook, while others prefer the information river of Twitter or the career-focused content more native to LinkedIn. Some prefer to look at pictures and pithy memes on Instagram, while others just like liking things in the public way that Pinterest makes possible. Then of course there are all those gadgets and appliances—there are 2.8 billion currently installed in the United States—that fall under the category of the Internet of Things (e.g., Fitbit, Jawbone, or smart home devices like Nest; for more on this see Chapter 6), designed not only to make your life easier but also to feed your information to companies who use it for marketing, research, and product development. Virtually all of these devices invite you to share your personal information not just with their app but with the world as well, via social media. Often, the devices come pre-set to share everything with everyone, and you can only maintain your privacy if you change the right settings.

Every milestone achieved on your healthy lifestyle wearable, entered on a fitness website, or logged on a phone-based app; every hour logged sleeping and talking and watching television; every time your smart appliance makes you coffee or turns on the morning news—all of that is tracked, and, depending on the company, either comes with a default setting to tell your friends and followers on social media your every move as related to that device, or includes an easy way to share those things.

#AlexFromTarget would have remained a humble checkout boy with a hip haircut had it not been for Twitter and Tumblr. He's one of the few examples of someone who found an upside to social media—and troll me all you want, but I maintain that this upside does only apply to a few select users, even if we point to the growing army of microcelebrity, mega YouTubers or the assorted superaccounts on this or that platform. Even with all the stars launched on social media, including Justin Bieber, the odds that you're benefiting from your profile remain miniscule.

Like a Justin Bieber also-ran, Alex Lee's odd luck put him within easy reach of fame and fortune. But that's not how it usually works. Generally, social media serves only as a time-suck and an open door through which any bad player can glean what's needed to steal your identity.

Social media makes you vulnerable to identity thieves in ways that most people aren't thinking about. They all know that some of their "friends" may be weirdos, or possibly even criminals—but even so, they still put their personal information where it can be seen by those "friends." It defies logic.

In a SUNY–Buffalo study published in 2014, Facebook users were asked about a phenomenon called farcing—friending a target with a fake account that looks like it comes from someone they know. Most of the users they talked to were aware of the dangers—that among all those they counted as Facebook friends, there were possibly a few scammers—but that understanding didn't have a big effect on the ways they used the site. The underlying belief was that financial harm (or worse) wouldn't come about as a result of their information being on the site. (It's important to bear in mind that while the focus in the above study was on Facebook, farcing happens on every social media platform.)

Unfortunately, we know this to be a false assumption. Identity thieves do not need much of your personal information to scam you, and what they need may be in the "about" silo of your timeline. It could be in a tagged photo, or, as we saw in the *Science* study on unicity and the reidentification of anonymized data, it could be a picture of your lunch or cocktail on Instagram coupled with a tweet or Facebook status update that provides that last piece of the puzzle that a scammer needs to access your credit.

Tag, You're It!

Let's say you're on Facebook, and you have set the privacy of every single shred of shareable information on your timeline as tightly as possible—you still may not be completely safe from prying eyes.

If you are tagged in a status update or a photograph, every single one of the tagger's "friends" can see the post. Presumably, the tag was put there because the post is either a picture of you (knowing what you look like is helpful information for a would-be identity thief) or the content represents something that you're interested in—which makes you an easier target for other scams like phishing, vishing, and smishing, since a scammer will know what subject lines and URLs you're more likely to click on if they come in the perfectly pitched text or email, which can both be spoofed to look like they are coming from someone you know.

Under "Account Settings," you can control how you are tagged and who can see the content you're tagged in. Choose the option that allows you to preapprove tags. Whether you do this to make sure nothing gets posted to Facebook that you wouldn't want colleagues at work to see, or to protect against the prying eyes of a scam artist, it's a good idea.

A few years ago I read a story about a newly instituted (and quickly suspended) employment screening policy of the Maryland Department of Public Safety and Correctional Services. There was the usual stuff you might expect in the job seeking process—you had to complete an application that included a bunch of personally identifiable information—but there was an extra piece of information requested that gave one applicant pause: The Maryland Department of Public Safety and Correctional Services had requested his Facebook username and password.

Robert Collins had previously worked for the department. He took a leave of absence after his mother died, and when that came to an end he applied for a job at another facility under the oversight of the corrections department. This process involved being recertified for employment in a job that involved regular contact with criminals. It was an admittedly sensitive hire, and the employer in this instance really did have to do a good job screening potential hires. The wrong person could cause serious problems, ranging from the proliferation of illegal substances within prison walls to smuggling prisoners weapons to aiding and abetting an escape.

The Internet ages *very* fast, and by any measure, 2011 was a very long time ago in the realm of things digital. But the behavior that Collins reported was inexcusable even at the time. According to Collins, his interviewer did not ask for, but rather demanded, his Facebook username and password.

Now, imagine you need a job. You know the process is winding down to a last sanity check—where the prospective employer calls a few people to make sure you're not a loony—and then you'll get an offer. You can tell. Now, imagine you're sitting in an office waiting for them to make that next move, and instead you get this curveball: "Do you mind if we poke around your Facebook account?" What would you do? If you are like a lot of people, including Robert Collins, you're going to hand over the keys to your Facebook account, or whatever other account the gatekeeper asks to see. The interview process is intense. You've gotten this far. It's simply too hard to find a job, and the stress is too great not to acquiesce to such a request— no matter how wrong it seems—when the alternative is not getting the job offer. And you are pretty careful about what you post, right? There aren't any embarrassing pictures of you. What about your private messages? Are you careful there, too?

So what happened at Mr. Collins's interview?

"He logged into my account and went through my pages, my posts, my messages, all my pictures, things like that," Collins told a reporter, not long after it happened. This private affair had become a news story because, immediately following the interview, Collins contacted the American Civil Liberties Union. When the

ACLU got in touch with the Department of Corrections about the incident, the explanation demonstrated two things: that no one there had thought much about the parameters native to privacy and social media—much less about best practices—and that they didn't really understand why requesting login information might be a problem.

If I had to guess, I'd say there was a question on the application about social media (i.e., do you use it?), and if the answer was yes, the follow-up gave the option of providing an applicant's login information "for screening purposes." In other words, it was yet another one of those "voluntary" items that an employer can review—like your credit report or a drug test—to determine if they should hire you. And once asked for their information, who wouldn't feel some pressure to say yes? Doubtless there would be plenty of applicants willing to hand over the keys to their likes, dislikes, and online behavior—including the way it chronicles their behavior in real life.

The point is that it's not okay for an organization to say, "We didn't think through the ramifications," and call it a day. We're somewhere on the Oregon Trail when it comes to Internet security, and many organizations have been behaving like bandits. And make no mistake, there has been a huge expansion of what's knowable about a person over the past decade or so, and it owes a lot to the explosive growth of social media. What hasn't evolved (or at least improved) is our sense of where the boundaries between public and private should be set. The tendency for most of us is to feel numb about it all. According to the November 2014 survey conducted by the Pew Research Center mentioned earlier in Chapter 6, "91% of adults in the survey 'agree' or 'strongly agree' that consumers have lost control over how personal information is collected and used by companies."

It makes perfect sense that employers would see the proliferation of personal information as a way to inform hiring decisions and staff up more efficiently. Why wouldn't they, if prospective workers don't complain, and the company benefits? It's the same tug of war between common sense and temptation that seems to occur on countless social media accounts every nanosecond of the day. According to the IACP (International Association of Chiefs of Police) Center for Social Media, there are more than 243,000 photographs posted to Facebook alone every minute. Worldwide, users log more than 3,125,000 likes per minute. The stats are impressive. What is both remarkable and still more disconcerting is the way that social media desensitizes users to the perils of public sharing.

The problem with handing over your username and password to a prospective employer—or really anyone—should be obvious. If it's not obvious, consider similar gambits. Should a potential employer get to interview a job candidate's spouse or partner? How about their siblings? Parents? Should they get to see your online dating profile? Or your personal email? Can they silently grade you on your grammar, your spending habits, and your friendships?

Thankfully, Collins's story is less common these days. Maryland, along with nineteen other states, has made it illegal for an employer to access an applicant's social media accounts. Back in 2011, the Maryland Department of Public Safety and Correctional Services said the policy was an attempt at better screening. By looking at an applicant's Facebook account, it would be possible to determine if he or she had any gang affiliations or family members incarcerated in the system.

It was just one of countless overreaches that occur with any new opportunity—especially one that revolves around useable data. Depending on your settings on Facebook, even employers without your login information can still see what you're like, and if you have good grammar. It goes without saying that Twitter is an open book unless you are protecting your tweets. There are, in fact, settings to protect your posts on all the major sites, but the real question is why would anyone, given the risks, want to post anything personal online?

Here's the deal: There is already way too much information about all of us out there just waiting to be found and exploited at our expense. Sometimes the exposure of information is intentional—you post pictures, you name family members, celebrate birthdays, attend school reunions—and sometimes you're oblivious to the slow leak of your personal information into the cybersphere. Regardless, we're all shedding a lot of personal identifying information just by dint of being a member of society. Our transactions on social media and beyond need to become more of a focus if we want to avoid having our lives turned upside down by an identity-related crime—we need to keep the focus on controlling what we can, and never lose sight of the fact that it's anyone's guess where our information may be.

According to Consumer Reports, more than 85 percent of Americans oppose online ad trackers that gather their personally identifiable information, and it doesn't matter if it's anonymized. Nobody trusts that their information is safe, and contrary to some industry-funded studies, most people are not comfortable with the sacrifice

> More than 80 percent of divorce lawyers say they mine social media sites to strengthen their cases against their clients' spouses.

of privacy on the altar of convenience. But while we are quick to gripe about ad tracking and the gathering of our data, even by places like the IRS that absolutely need it, there we are, clicking and pecking away on our keyboards, trained on little boxes asking us to tell the world what's on our minds. It really does seem insane.

I do have one thought for those who insist on the real-time documentation of life. My former press secretary at New Jersey's Division of Consumer Affairs, Larry Nagy, used to call it the "*60 Minutes*" theory.

Larry's advice: "Don't do anything"—and here I would insert, "or type anything"—"that, if on a Sunday evening, when you're eating your TV dinner in front of your television set, and Mike Wallace came on *60 Minutes* and told you about you, would prevent you from finishing your dinner."

No one has a greater stake in our future and economic security than we do. That means we need to be ever vigilant, self-aware, and, above all, careful. Even if no one ever asks for your social media and login information, that doesn't mean someone (on their own behalf or that of another) is not looking through your pages, posts, messages, pictures, and Facebook wall as you read this, and you need to assume that's the case. As a company, Facebook's mission is not to be a personal journal or an archive of your correspondence. Their mission is to collect your personal information and sell it to advertisers—that's it. They get you to hand it over by giving you access to a lifetime's worth of friends and memories. It's a seductive proposition, and you may decide that it's worth it. Just be careful, because it comes at a price.

Getting a Handle on the Apocalypse

@federalreserve and @CENTCOM exist on Twitter. Why? Your guess is as good as mine. But it's true; they're there—and they have almost 400,000 followers between them. While the upside is unclear—most of the tweets are about banal scheduling items and the public face of current military operations—the downside is a world crisis caused by 140 characters or less.

Earlier this year, the Twitter account of U.S. Central Command was hacked. The first tweet went out at 12:30 p.m. eastern time and said, "AMERICAN SOLDIERS, WE ARE COMING, WATCH YOUR BACK. ISIS." The account was suspended.

It takes time to mobilize troops, so panic was relatively easy to prevent in that case. But what if the panic was financial? It might happen too fast to prevent. What happens when someone gets hold of @federalreserve and posts a message like this: "New Fed figures fuel inflation fears—discount rate will be set at 25% next week"?

It has been five years since Mark Zuckerberg declared that the age of privacy was over. He was in a position to know, because he was the one ending it.

The wild pronouncements of an unstoppable force of nature worth billions of dollars notwithstanding, many of us still care about our privacy, and if we choose to protect it, we can. Privacy is not dead, but to some extent it's going underground. The cattle call of data megabreaches now includes the world's largest companies and most powerful governments. When Sony Pictures and Centcom can get hacked—and they are just two obvious examples—one has to assume that Facebook is hackable, too. For legions of hackers, the social media giant is the white whale. If our operating theory holds true, that everyone and everything is vulnerable and it's just a matter of time before it gets got—then news of Facebook's breach is coming. And when it does, it won't be pretty.

Consider what would happen if a file about you, one that would put to shame anything that the CIA could have amassed (because you sourced it yourself), a dossier with not only your personally identifiable information, but everything that makes you unique, suddenly was out there, available to the highest bidder. Bear in mind, whoever got your file would also have a pretty good idea of how much money you make, and thus would be able to take maximum advantage of your identity.

A huge percentage of Americans don't think that Facebook is using their personal information fairly. Yet there we are, keeping up with friends and family; spying on enemies or former significant others; checking out the latest tragedy in some faraway place or right next door; watching cute animal videos, amazing child performers, or various acts of political chicanery; or ogling the beach photos of our prom dates from 1974.

One option is to do something that Mark Zuckerberg has derided as inauthentic. You can alternate between a number of different Facebook accounts, migrating from one to the next every

Facebook Doesn't Have Stringent Authentication

When Facebook acquired Instagram, it asked users who forgot their passwords to upload pictures of a government-issued photo ID by way of authentication. What happens when—not if—there is a breach and that invaluable piece of information gets into the wrong hands?

Why doesn't Facebook use the same authentication protocols as banks and credit agencies? Certainly with revenue of $3.85 billion—up from $2.59 billion the prior year—Facebook can afford it. And it's in their interest. Without your personally identifiable information, they would be worth nowhere near as much as they are. Your PII is worth a lot more than your bank information to a thief who knows how to use it.

couple of months. If Facebook's game plan is to get an accurate picture of you, they will be foiled, confronted with a cubist version worthy of a modern art museum or a hall of mirrors. While it's far from foolproof, this strategy is at least one way to prepare for a potential megabreach of any major social networking site, since it will be harder for a third party to piece together your identity and use it. It's a lifehack to protect your privacy and personal information.

We've already discussed the fact that identity thieves like to work close to home—often targeting immediate family, relatives, and close friends. More than 30 percent of all reported identity-related crimes fall under this category. So it follows that you may be Facebook friends with some aspiring identity thieves, and they may be real people for whom you will have mixed feelings if they ever take the plunge and try to victimize you. But there is another, related threat on Facebook. Farcing is simple. Just as friends and family use proximity to get the information they need to scam you, people on Facebook create farce accounts pretending to be a friend, or more commonly someone pretending to be the friend of a friend, and, once within your circle of trust, they can gather all the information needed to scam you, depending on how you have your profile set up. Potentially, that would include your legal name, date of birth, where you grew up and went to school, any colleges you might have attended, family members, favorite vacation spots, vacation plans, nicknames, pet names, and so on. While you should set up your account so that, in the event there's a breach at Facebook, your information will not be very useful to an identity thief, the present threat of farcing is a very good reason to be careful.

If you don't have the time to maintain multiple Facebook accounts, here are seven things you can do to at least minimize the damage when Facebook gets hacked.

1. Change your name.

If you tweak your name just a little, or use a nickname, life will be easier for you after a potential hack. Open more than one account. Yes, it violates Facebook's terms of service, but 80 million accounts already do it, says privacy expert John Sileo. And don't be scared by the argument that anonymity leads to crime, says online security expert C. Matthew Curtin: "You can do bad things anonymously, and you can do bad things using your name."

2. Stop geotagging your photos.

Geotagging includes the latitude and longitude where a picture was taken, that is, home. If you right-click on a photo, you can find this information under "properties." If you are using an iPhone, look under "Settings," go to "Privacy," then "Location Services" to turn off location services for all applications or just for individual applications, like the camera. Even if you turn this feature off on your camera or smartphone, all photos you have already taken will contain the information.

3. Lie about your age.

While it's fun to get birthday greetings on your wall, your birth date is a key piece of information needed to steal your identity. At least post the wrong year.

4. Don't store your credit card information on the site.

Facebook has several services that require a credit card. Buyer beware.

5. Have some boundaries.

When Facebook asks you where your photo was taken, keep it to yourself. There is no reason to post pictures that tell a potential thief not only where your house is, but what sort of transportation will be needed to take all your stuff. Don't brag about new cars, especially if your photos show where you keep the keys in your kitchen. And set your privacy controls so only people you know can see factoids that could be used to create a new credit card account or the like.

6. Less is more (peace of mind).

While we all have pride in the things we've done and the places we've lived, the more you tell the world about it, the more likely that information will bring you to the attention of an identity thief. Go through your timeline and remove posts that provide personally identifiable information.

7. Deactivate your account.

As Mr. Miyagi told Daniel-san in *The Karate Kid*, "Remember, best block, no be there." You can't get hacked if you don't have an account.

The threat of farcing should be sufficient to suggest that there is a major downside to sharing too much information online, above and beyond the danger of a huge security breach. There is no wisdom in placing so much trust and personal data in the hands of such a mercurial company that again and again has shown that it has a cavalier attitude toward your privacy.

With more than 1 billion users—the world's largest repository of consumer likes and dislikes in the global marketplace—Facebook is going to continue strip-mining that treasure trove comprised of your data. But if the megabreaches of the past few years have proven anything, it is that nothing is safe.

The age of privacy is dead. Long live the age of privacy!

An identity thief can make life very difficult for you. As the Twitter hack proves, it's only a matter of time. And how can anyone in their right mind "Like" that?

10

From Dangerous to Deadly

On Healthcare Scams and Medical Identity Theft

Does the name Davey Scatino ring any bells? You may not remember him by name. On the long-running HBO series *The Sopranos*, he is Tony's childhood friend—a troubled guy who owns a sporting goods store and gets in way over his head with gambling debt. For those who didn't watch the show, Davey learns the hard way that financial obligations have to be met, regardless of the longstanding bonds of friendship, and with all the more alacrity when the person carrying the debt is an emotionally complex mob boss. (For the record, Tony warns him to stay away from the high-stakes executive game.)

Davey's dilemma introduced a wide viewership to the concept of a "bust-out." The term has two meanings, both of them negative. In cards, you bust out when you lose all your chips. (In other words, you're out of the game.) In the organized crime version, the "chips" are someone's spending power—whether it takes the form of credit or unused medical coverage doesn't much matter. When a crime boss orders a bust-out, he's talking about cashing in on *everything* a person owns that can be converted quickly into cold, hard cash. (Tony ends up with Davey's SUV and his sporting goods store, and Davey loses a lot more.) In mobspeak, the "mark," or victim, is generally someone who has run afoul of the boss. In real life, victims are chosen by the Dumb Luck Lottery system. You never know when your (Social Security) number is going to come up, but the odds are good you will be thoroughly screwed when it does. And when it comes to a medical coverage bust-out, doctors, hospitals, and laboratories are just about as patient as a crime boss. That means you have to pay up now and sort out the mistake after the fact if you want to keep your credit intact.

In the pioneer days of identity theft, fraudsters were more interested in grabbing credit card numbers, hijacking money-related accounts, and engaging in the occasional quasi-exotic financial crime linked to a person's personally identifiable information. While tax refund diversion has become all the rage over the past few years, raiding healthcare coverage can also be very lucrative—and with the aid of a crooked doctor willing to treat a nonexistent cancer or replace every joint in a patient's body, there's a fortune to be made.

According to the Centers for Medicare and Medicaid Services (CMS), "U.S. healthcare spending grew 3.6 percent in 2013, reaching $2.9 trillion or $9,255 per person. As a share of the nation's Gross Domestic Product, health spending accounted for 17.4 percent." *Forbes Magazine* pegged total healthcare spending in 2013 at $3.8 trillion, and, citing CMS and other projections from Deloitte, projected that that number would hit $5 trillion or more by 2022.

> Medical identity theft and other healthcare-related scams are easier to do than some of the older, more established ways crooks made bank (excuse the pun), and they carry less prison time (if any).

That's a huge pile of money, and it attracts all kinds of attention—not all of it good.

This sector is simply too delicious for organized crime to overlook. Healthcare fraud involves significantly more bad actors than just dishonest healthcare providers. "So enticing an invitation is our nation's ever-growing pool of healthcare money," an article on the National Health Care Anti-Fraud Association website reports, "that in certain areas—Florida, for example—law enforcement agencies and health insurers have witnessed in recent years the migration of some criminals from illegal drug trafficking into the safer and far more lucrative business of perpetrating fraud schemes against Medicare, Medicaid and private health insurance companies." It is striking to think that identity theft in this realm is more lucrative than smuggling cocaine, but it's true. Medical data sells for as much as ten times what financial data fetches on the data black markets of the dark web, and there is so much money out there for healthcare that it makes pretty much every other kind of crime seem pretty small-time.

Picture a lush field of wheat ready to be harvested. Now, imagine all that wheat is available cash—whether it takes the form of credit lines or available healthcare coverage doesn't really matter: It all converts to cash easily enough. What do you suppose happens to a giant field full of money? You can put up all the fences you want, but sooner or later someone is going to come for it. And if they're smart, they'll bust it out for every last penny.

Different kinds of bust-outs are in play whenever we talk about medical identity theft and healthcare-related fraud. They can involve accomplices in the form of imposter patients, greedy doctors, or both—TV-ready characters crushed by the weight of their flaws, empty husks of people with a medical degree or a crooked doctor friend, and suffocating debt who get mixed up with the wrong crowd.

The scam could be anything. In a recent New York City scam, homeless people with valid Medicaid cards were ferried around the outer boroughs of the Bronx and Brooklyn to see podiatrists who "diagnosed" them with fictitious maladies that required expensive hardware like orthotics. The scammers kept the money paid out by Medicaid, and the homeless victims were given discounted sneakers and boots, which they could choose in a storeroom described as being "like a shoe store."

Batteries of needless tests and remedies were "performed" in a pantomime of real medicine, then billed out on the Medicaid cards of those homeless people targeted. Prosecutors estimate the total windfall for that sham was around $7 million, which doesn't include possible hits on those patients' accounts after the fact. And unfortunately, while the above story was featured in the headlines recently, the scam itself has been around for a while. A common variation on this theme takes the form of "free lunch" offers for seniors, where sandwiches and soda are just starters for the main course: the Medicare information of unwitting retirees, which is gobbled up by fraudsters and used to generate payment on bogus bills.

Charles Piper, an investigator working out of Tennessee, discovered a typical racket at a psychological care facility where patients with Alzheimer's disease were herded into a small room with a television set for treatment. Perhaps it was a memory exercise, because they were shown the same movie over and over. It was a simple fraud. Each time the patients watched *Forrest Gump*, their insurance was billed for group therapy.

While that's a straightforward scam, there can be a variety of scenarios. For instance, none of the patients corralled for treatment have Alzheimer's disease. Easier yet, imagine no room and no patients, but seven envelopes, each with a neatly folded explanation of benefits listing group therapy sessions, heading to seven states and destined for the mailboxes of seven people who don't suffer from Alzheimer's.

Some of the older stories will be familiar to those who follow medical identity theft news, such as two reported in the *New York Times*. One victim was Brandon Sharp, who was thirty-seven years old and living in Houston when he first learned about a $19,000 bill for a helicopter ambulance ride that he never took.

The Scam

They were two bills for seemingly benign medical charges, one for a semen analysis and the other a pregnancy test. But here's a twist: It appeared that both tests were performed on the same day, on the same person. Strange? It gets stranger. She was a seventy-two-year-old grandmother.

According IDT911, beginning in 2006, June Smith's personal information—including her Social Security number—was used to charge Medicare for tens of thousands of dollars of medical services in her name. She discovered the charges because she carefully reviewed all explanation of benefits statements that she received. Otherwise neither she nor the Medicare folks would have been the wiser. According to Ms. Smith, even though she tried to bring this to the attention of officials, Medicare paid the bills. Neither Ms. Smith nor her husband incurred any charges as a result of the fraud, but they were very concerned they would hit a Medicare benefits cap and ultimately be denied access to legitimate services in the future.

Because she had identity theft services through her homeowner's insurance policy, she was helped by a professional fraud

There were other emergency room visits in cities he'd never been, but he didn't learn about them until he requested a copy of his credit report in preparation for a mortgage application.

The other, more publicized story mentioned in the 2009 *Times* article happened in Naples, Florida, three years earlier. At the time, the strain of fraud was entirely new. Fernando Ferrer Jr., a twenty-nine-year-old from Naples who owned a company called Advanced Medical Claims, conspired with his cousin, twenty-two-year-old Isis Machado, who worked the front desk at the Cleveland Clinic and, over a one-year period, downloaded and printed out information—Medicare beneficiary numbers, Social Security numbers, dates of birth, and other sensitive data—belonging to investigator. After an exhaustive investigation, it was determined that many of the supposed doctors and medical entities making the charges weren't licensed or operating as legitimate businesses. They appeared to be fictitious people and institutions created by scammers who feasted off government benefits. After complaining for several years, she ultimately received a letter from Medicare stating that one group of charges was considered fraudulent and would not be paid. It was an ordeal that lasted over four years.

In an interview with WABC-TV's "7 on Your Side," she advised other seniors, "It's important for people like me to have their eyes open."

"Why are you paying these bills?" Smith once asked a Medicare representative, after explaining her situation.

According to Ms. Smith, the customer rep responded, "Because they come to us."

The lesson: Anytime you receive an explanation of benefits statement, read it. If you find an error, bring it to the attention of the medical provider or the insurer. If they won't respond, get a professional to help.

1,100 patients. Ferrer used that information to rack up more than $2.8 million in fraudulent bills paid out by Medicare.

Something akin to this can happen when a fraudster uses your personally identifiable information in the commission of a crime in the medical and healthcare areas.

> The money available for healthcare is a bust-out waiting to happen—in fact, scratch that: It's already happening.

In 2014, over the span of just one year, we witnessed the massive growth of a serious problem in the health industry. For an umbrella category, call it "data insecurity." Nearly 100 million healthcare-related records were breached in 2014 (most of which we learned about in early 2015). In every case, the compromised records included the stuff of identity theft nightmares: addresses (both virtual and actual), phone numbers, birth dates, and Social Security numbers. There was enough sensitive information in these breaches to make possible any type of identity-related scam out there.

Anthem fumbled nearly 80 million personal records, Tennessee-based Community Health Systems was sacked for a loss of another 4.5 million, and, of course, there was the Premera breach, with its 11 million exposed individuals marking the largest-ever breach of patient medical records.

Unlike the Anthem and Community Health Systems breaches, because the Premera compromise included medical records, it opened the door to much more serious kinds of fraud (extortion leading the list) and identity-related scams.

Medical records contain the most confidential kinds of information about us. The data leaked by Premera was of a far more revealing and personal nature than the kinds of personal information usually involved in a breach. Your medical records may contain information you'd never want people to know—quite possibly things that could cost you a job or a relationship. Worse, if you are one of the 11 million people affected by the Premera breach, it exists out there in databases that you cannot control, and the possibility that the information in those stolen files will come back to bite you is permanent.

One hypothetical but not too far-fetched danger here is the creation of a more systematized approach to medical identity theft that would be more akin to the way credit card data is sold on the deep web. With that comes the potential for a much more complex and hard to unravel strain of identity theft. Since all of a patient's history is available, thieves could potentially create an index to match every conceivable point of differentiation such as blood type, allergy, and gender. The ability to match medical history to potential imposter would lessen the possibility of being

From WikiLeaks

On Thursday, April 30[, 2009], the secure site for the Virginia Prescription Monitoring Program (PMP) was replaced with a $US10M ransom demand:

"I have your shit! In *my* possession, right now, are 8,257,378 patient records and a total of 35,548,087 prescriptions. Also, I made an encrypted backup and deleted the original. Unfortunately for Virginia, their backups seem to have gone missing, too. Uhoh :(For $10 million, I will gladly send along the password."

foiled by duplicated procedures (you can't have three hip replacements), or getting caught because medical information was changed in the scammed person's account and they got sick or died as a result. This really could be the medical equivalent of selling credit card data on the black market by ZIP code.

The U.S. Office of Personnel Management (OPM) is responsible for posting federal job listings and conducting background checks on prospective employees; it manages pension benefits and makes sure that the federal workplace maintains an environment where hard work and excellent performance are rewarded. It is the federal government's human resources department. As such, the OPM is also responsible for making sure that healthcare benefits for federal employees are up to par. Had Premera paid attention to the OPM's report sent to them on April 18, 2014, more than three weeks before they suffered the catastrophic loss of medical records belonging to more than 11 million customers, perhaps the story would have been different.

What was in that report? The OPM told Premera that its network security procedures were inadequate. The audit report went on at some length, detailing the situation Premera faced, and then provided ten recommendations to fix existing problems. The document was crystal clear: the vulnerabilities exposed the healthcare network to the possibility of a breach. Its security was insufficient, and sensitive personally identifiable information was in danger of being stolen by hackers. Premera didn't respond to the audit until June 30, nearly two months after the May 5 breach. Their response said that the company had made some changes, and that they would investigate and implement fixes for the remaining issues by the end of 2014.

Post-breach, in response to reporters' questions, Premera spokesman Eric Earling said, "We believe the questions OPM raised in their routine audit are separate from this sophisticated cyberattack." Sure, but isn't that always the case? When a big company gets compromised—no matter how simple the hack—it's Public Relations 101 to claim that the company couldn't have seen it coming. The hackers, these organizations like to say, are just too smart.

As it stands, there are several class-action lawsuits pending against Premera for failure to maintain security, and for the resulting harm to its members' personal data security. The lawsuits were all filed in Seattle at the U.S. District Court. The customers filing suit hail from Washington, Nevada, and Massachusetts. The complaints hinge on a few basic items: that Premera was negligent and thus was in breach of contract with end users, that the company violated the Washington Consumer Protection Act, and that too much time passed between the date the company knew there had been a breach—January 29, 2015—and when they actually told customers about it almost three months later.

But no matter how much money is awarded—a seemingly impossible number to determine—no financial windfall can eliminate the risks of having your personal data exposed.

It used to be that the crimes associated with medical identity theft were hard to detect and resolve because of the nature of the records, which were often offline in a filing cabinet. If you didn't know the name of the doctor who provided care to your impostter, that was the end of it. But even though files now live online, it is still no easier. Files can be widely dispersed on networks that aren't connected, meaning that there is no way to determine if parts of a person's medical history exist in more than one place, or if a patient's file is connected to different names, blood types, allergies, or other medical data.

> When it comes to these scams, they want your money and your life—or, at the very least, the bad guys don't care if you break out in hives.

According to the World Privacy Forum's groundbreaking 2006 study that first revealed the threat of medical identity theft, "victims of medical identity theft do not have the right to prevent healthcare providers, medical clearinghouses, or insurers from reporting and re-reporting information that has resulted from identity theft."

Whether it is because credit card companies have gotten better at manning the ramparts or there is just too much of an upside in identity-related healthcare fraud, medical identity-type malfeasance is definitely on the rise. And sometimes acts of healthcare fraud don't seem identity-related at first blush, but secretly are.

Eva Casey Velasquez, president and CEO of the Identity Theft Resource Center, explained the situation well: "Frauds and scams are identity-related even if during the initial scam the victim only parts with money or is used to cause a third party or entity to part with it, and the reason for this is that generally victims also part with personally identifiable information in the process of being scammed or defrauded. Then months later, the other shoe drops and they discover that they've become identity theft victims as well."

According to Bloomberg Business, medical identity theft alone increased nearly 22 percent in 2014. The increase was attributed to the ever-growing reliance on digital recordkeeping in the medical world and the healthcare industry with which it communicates. In 2014 alone, more than a half million people were victimized by disreputable companies set up to commit fraud, or by medical practitioners engaged in various kinds of insurance fraud. This includes administering care, knowingly or not, to imposter patients stealing healthcare by using an identity theft victim's particulars. The Ponemon Institute reported that the average cost to a victim of this kind of crime was a whopping $13,500.

Where did all that money go? For the most part, it paid medical bills for services that were never rendered to the actual patient (who got charged regardless).

Sometimes something happened only on paper, or services were provided to an impostor patient who stole or bought healthcare credentials in order to get treatment—and the bills were sent to the victim or, more commonly, to a collection agency that subsequently reported their loss to the three credit reporting agencies. In addition to paying bills for fraudulent services and having their credit reports suffer for years, victims are often saddled with high legal fees.

The average amount of time spent on resolving a case of medical identity theft or fraud, according to the Ponemon Institute, was two hundred hours in 2014. Addressing false entries on your medical record is not easy, and often entries cannot be entirely resolved, depending on the type of information and how it's been distributed and stored by subsequent parties. So, if someone were to use your insurance to get treatment for, say, a sexually transmitted disease or a serious psychiatric disorder, that may well stay in your files and cause you problems down the line. That leads to another problem, namely, that erroneous information on a person's medical record can impact their reputation, and, with that, potentially harm their ability to secure employment.

But the most important statistic is one that doesn't get nearly enough attention. Nineteen percent of medical identity theft

**From Pam Dixon's Study, *Medical Identity Theft:
The Information Crime That Can Kill You*, Published in 2006
by the World Privacy Forum**

Perhaps the most egregious victim stories in this area come from
a Boston area psychiatrist who altered his patients' records and
others' records in order to make money from fraudulent billing.
The psychiatrist, a certain Dr. Skodnek, gave diagnoses of severe
depression and in some cases drug addiction and abuse to people
who weren't even his patients. The psychiatrist billed insurance
companies for these services. Court documents from the case
describe the harms:

> There is no reason to believe that this misinformation will not
> lead to misfortune for those whose names Skodnek used in
> fabricating the sessions. This is an information age. While
> nominally confidential, these records are vulnerable to disclo-
> sure to any number of sources. Whether it should or not, the
> misinformation will almost certainly have an impact on patients'
> lives. It may determine whether an individual will be given a
> health insurance policy; it may decide whether he or she will
> receive government clearance; it may affect a whole host of other
> situations. . . . Dr. Skodnek's abuse of trust—and its unquestion-
> able impact on his patients' lives and the lives of their family
> members—are very, very troubling. And, what is unusual about
> this fraud scheme is not that Dr. Skodnek "puffed" the time he
> spent but went much, much further. He created a paper trail for
> these patients out of whole cloth, inventing histories of mental
> health treatment with which those individuals must now contend.

This case is the best-documented chronicle of this kind of harm.
However, many victims of medical identity theft may have similar
issues, they just haven't learned about them yet.

Denial of Insurance

Victims of medical identity theft can be denied insurance due to
imposter activity. In the Skodnek case, the doctor used up each

family member's insurance one after the other until the benefits were "capped."

Loss of Reputation

When a medical file has been altered by a suspect, it becomes an albatross around the victim's neck. A judge in the Skodnek case wrote:

> The evidence suggests that once the claims were entered they cannot be deleted from the system. The most that can be done is to enter a notation in the computer records to reflect that a particular claim was false. In order to accomplish this, each member is obliged to write to Blue Cross/Blue Shield disputing the individual records. Moreover, even where a notation is entered to show that the billing record was false, the insurance carrier cannot declare—and the notation will thus not reflect—whether Skodnek's statements about diagnosis, medications prescribed and/or psychiatric symptoms of the patient were false.

This is true. After falsified information is entered into a patient file, that information is typically in that file for good. Most health-care providers, upon learning of a mistake, will correct the file. But not all.

victims reported erroneous information attached to their medical histories—in some cases, fraud-related entries that were at odds with allergies or preexisting conditions or maladies, information that could lead to medically incorrect treatment or even life-threatening decisions being made by an unwitting doctor. The oddities that get dropped into a victim's permanent medical files can be very hard to remove, and they can be harmful in a variety of ways.

Pam Dixon's seminal study on medical identity theft is a key document for people who make it their business to attack the identity theft problem. It shined a bright light in particular on the issue of medical identity theft, and was where I first read about the various cases that she had tracked down, largely sourced from the Federal Trade Commission's Consumer Sentinel Hotline in 2006. Although dated, they are representative of the problem:

According to one victim, "On March 20, 2006, someone used my Social Security number at the Primary Diagnostic Clinic at Duke University to obtain medical services and I was billed for these services. The individual did not show proof of insurance or any type of ID. I have never been a patient at any Duke facility so the bill was quite a surprise."

Another individual stated that someone "keeps putting in a change of address for him but he is not doing it." This consumer also received two medical bills for a regional medical center on his credit report that were not his.

One consumer describes a nightmare of identity theft red tape: "Back in 1995 my wallet was stolen at a nearby convenience store in Elsa, Texas. There were no problems at that time until I tried to do my income tax return. They put it on hold because somebody was using my Social Security Number to work in another state . . . I have also been denied credit card accounts, loans, and have been charged with accounts from another state. There is one account that I have received from Sterling ER Physicians for the amount of $339 from a collection agency that is from Trenton, New Jersey. I have never left the state of Texas . . . and the person who is using my Social Security Number is receiving medical treatment."

After a car burglary, a Kentucky consumer had seven accounts opened by an imposter. The imposter received treatment at a hospital; the bills went to collections. A consumer found his father's personal information in his own accounts, including new medical bills and new credit card bills.

One consumer who looked at her credit report found that an imposter using her information had rented an apartment and had obtained medical services at a Washington, DC, hospital, as well as a wireless account.

A Texas consumer, after receiving her credit report, found out that the suspect had used her Social Security number at a regional medical center for $1,650 worth of medical treatment. Her Social Security card had been stolen.

An Arizona man discovered two bills on his credit report that were not his—but were listed in his name. He suspected his ex-wife may have been the culprit.

One consumer called to state that an imposter had used her identity to obtain a DirecTV account and to use services at a pathology lab. The medical account was turned over to collections, and debt collectors were actively trying to collect $790 from the victim.

A Connecticut consumer reported that someone obtained medical services at Yale–New Haven Hospital in their name, using their Social Security number. The consumer's checking account was also taken over by the imposter.

Stupid Things That Make Matters Worse

Ponemon's *Fourth Annual Benchmark Study on Patient Privacy and Data Security*, published in May 2014, reported that attacks on healthcare organizations increased by 100 percent over a four-year period. The study found fault with the Affordable Care Act and, more generally, with bad data-security practices at medical organizations—ranging from hospitals to insurers.

One practice singled out in particular was BYOD, or "bring your own device," practices. Doctors and other medical employees frequently need to access sensitive data electronically, and the practice of downloading it to their personal laptops, tablets, and smartphones presents significant problems.

"Despite concerns about employee negligence and the use of insecure mobile devices," the report found that "88 percent of organizations permit employees and medical staff to use their own mobile devices such as smart phones or tablets to connect to their organization's networks or enterprise systems such as email. Similar to last year more than half of (these) organizations are not confident that the personally-owned mobile devices or BYOD are secure."

The report was also crystal clear about the fact that very few organizations require their employees to install antivirus/antimalware software on their smartphones or tablets or scan and remove all mobile apps that present a security threat prior to allowing them to be connected to their networks or systems. And while the Ponemon study did not explore enforcement mechanisms, it is likely that even with organizations that did have some kind of protocol regarding BYOD and antivirus or antimalware software, self-policing is the rule. There is no way of knowing whether a given employee has downloaded every update, so protection against malware may be very spotty, even if on the surface it appears to be an issue on an organization's radar.

I don't know about you, but that scares me to death, because we live in a time when databases have started to include a terrifying amount of extremely intimate information about illnesses, diagnoses, treatments, and health issues that nobody should have to fear might become reading material for criminals or their customers.

So what happens if a criminal gets his or her hands on your pristine medical records? To some extent, it depends on how much information you have shared with your doctor. While it goes without saying that your physician will have all the requisite contact and insurance information for billing, he or she might also have information that they don't necessarily need, such as your Social Security number (if you are insured, your doctor probably does not need this information, and it's worth at least trying to persuade them to proceed without it). They also don't need a ton of personally identifiable information that falls under the category of TMI: the names and/or birthdays of family members (which often do double duty as passwords or security questions for your bank, credit card, and brokerage accounts). Some doctors and medical groups will even hold onto financial information that, in the wrong hands, could be used to access your bank or credit card accounts.

In addition to these financial risks, your medical records provide information that can be used in other ways. For instance, once a criminal has your personal information and insurance details, he or she can use it, or enable another person to use it, to gain access to the healthcare system in your name, and the result could be the contamination of your medical records with his or her comingled information. Nothing is more dangerous than going to a hospital and having "your" medical records, as used by an identity thief or his/her customer, reflect an inaccurate blood type, medical history, or the existence or absence of certain allergies as you are trying to access care, particularly in an emergency situation. If an impostor uses your insurance to gain access to healthcare, it can also affect your own ability to access care: many insurance plans have yearly caps on certain types of procedures and treatments—and no insurance company is going to pay for one person to have an appendectomy twice. An identity thief with access to your insurance could drain your coverage before you even know it's happened, and leave you in the lurch when you need it.

There is of course another big target here, namely, your prescription history. Prescription drug abuse continues its meteoric rise, and the value of some prescription drugs on the street, such as Oxycodone, is skyrocketing. An identity thief could very well use his or her access to your medical records to get the prescription drugs you need, leaving you both without medication and under suspicion for quickly maxing out your refills and trying to get more.

Massive cyberattacks that target credit and debit cards aren't anywhere near as problematic. In reality, once those cards are replaced, the immediate danger has passed, and there is rarely any burden for the cardholder. Subsequent phishing attacks by email, phone, and text are a bit more problematic, but if consumers exercise care—don't click on links that make no sense, and think about what might not make sense—damage can be contained, and any issues that do arise can be resolved. However, when it involves medical identity theft, the crime can be nearly invisible. If it is discovered at all, it's not until there's an emergency when the consequences can be literally life threatening. This is why it is important to carefully check every explanation of benefits that comes in the mail. Another practice: Ask to see your medical records whenever you visit your doctor or specialist.

11

Wanted Dead or Alive

(But It's Easier If You're Dead)

I don't want to achieve immortality through my work;
I want to achieve it by not dying.

—WOODY ALLEN

Death is not a fun topic for anyone, particularly for the deceased, which is precisely why this chapter begins with a line attributed to Woody Allen. The reason I've spread some humor throughout this chapter is simple: It's a morbid subject. If you are reading this section to get your bearings in the management of a loved one's estate, I hope you won't mistake any drollery or wordplay for disrespect. That said, the best eulogies make us laugh as much as they make us cry, but the various strains of identity theft (and scams) that can occur postmortem don't naturally make for stand-up comedy material.

At this point in our journey through the hell of identity theft, my guess is that you've had it with me pointing out that it is the third certainty in life. (It's right behind death and taxes, in case you just felt like diving into this chapter before reading the others and are thus hearing this for the first time.) And of course you'd be dead right if you felt that way. But this chapter is about the rare instance where you can experience all three certainties at once—the tax-related identity theft of a dead person.

There are a great many crimes that can be committed using different elements of someone's personally identifiable information

From 2006 through 2011, some 67,000 federal tax returns were filed where the names on the earnings reports didn't match the names associated with the Social Security numbers. They were worth $3.1 million.

While it might have been a bunch of bum guesses—since fraudsters do occasionally roll the dice with made-up SSNs—it is more likely that these criminals knew for a fact that those numbers hadn't been recorded on the Death Master File.

According to a 2015 report on CNN, employers made more than 4,000 E-Verify inquiries from 2008 to 2011 using nearly 3,900 SSNs belonging to people born before June 16, 1901.

after they die. Death is a game-ender when it comes to most types of criminal activity (it's hard to rob a bank or murder someone if you're six feet under). And for all practical purposes, death is a release from all contracts. But, as you will see later in this chapter, some of those contractual obligations, and certain kinds of crimes, have a tendency to linger a bit longer than they should.

Because the kind of crimes we're talking about take advantage of the lag time between death and the closing of an estate, the first and perhaps most important point I can make here is that you should factor the eventuality of postmortem identity theft into your estate planning. The crimes aren't committed against the decedent, per se, because not only is filing a complaint no longer an option for a deceased person, but he or she is technically no longer there to violate in the first place.

However, that's not the case in the eyes of the law. As far as the state, the federal government, and all the places where the decedent did business are concerned, he or she is still alive until the organizations concerned are officially notified that the deceased, who had been previously paying income tax, will now be paying an inheritance tax, having been transmogrified into an entity that most certainly can get got: namely, the decedent's estate.

When an estate gets hit, it definitely has a very negative effect on the survivors of the dearly departed. The mourning process is interrupted. Often, no one in the family has been invested with power of attorney, which means that financial crimes against the estate can't be stopped right away, much less sorted out. This is why it's so important to include postmortem identity theft precautions in your estate planning, which would include granting power of attorney to a trusted family member, one that the other beneficiaries know about, and making sure you have all postmortem communications ready (there are sample letters in Appendix 5), so that all your family needs to do is get the requisite copies of your official death certificate and distribute them in a timely fashion. Additionally, you can obviate a number of issues by doing something as simple as signing up for an identity theft protection program that includes identity management services as well as credit monitoring. Simple precautions can mean the difference between a relatively easy probate process and a big financial loss to further compound your emotional one.

With a wide gamut of opportunities, ranging from pillaging the decedent's credit to co-opting his or her identity (so that the dead figuratively—i.e., financially—walk again, at least in name and Social Security number), it is important that family members and their lawyers acquaint themselves with the threats out there. When it comes to identity theft, forewarned is forearmed.

Remember, you're going to get got. It might be happening as you read this sentence. If that's the case, it's something you will discover soon enough, because you are practicing the Three Ms and the fraud will turn up during your monitoring process while it's still a pending charge or a hard inquiry at one of the three credit reporting agencies. After you pass away, however, unless appropriate measures are taken, no one will be checking. You can set up transaction alerts on your credit cards—even order a credit freeze—but it doesn't matter. Your turn to get got might not come till you're pushing up daisies. In fact, one of the greatest times of vulnerability is immediately after death, precisely because no one is paying attention to the credit and identity issues of the deceased.

Depending on the postdeath scenario and the kinds of information involved, this particular variety of identity shenanigan can be an annoyance, or it can be an unholy combination of *Brewster's Millions* and *Night of the Living Dead*.

Here's what you need to know: Any identity thief worth his or her salt can get through your defenses. In fact, it's child's play for them. Obviously, transaction notifications are worthless, because they only work if someone is receiving them. But even if a relative has been designated to monitor your phone, email, and social networking, it's easy for an

> **Exercise Number One**
>
> 1. Take your driver's license out of your wallet.
> 2. Now look at the back of it.
> 3. Note there is no box to check for "Identity Donor."

information-laden crook to turn the notifications off. The same thing goes for a credit freeze. The fact is, all your fraud precautions can be undone with a few phone calls, provided the caller has enough personally identifiable information.

It's not something people tend to focus on very much. After all, why would anyone worry about the dead shopping for a loan? For the same reason, it may not occur to some folks that the decedent's credit cards, birth certificate, Social Security number, old tax documents, and the far-flung constellation of identifying information need to be collected and stored securely.

The reason you need to be so careful should be clear by now. The recently deceased continue to exist on paper, and this may well be the case for some time. Until the government has officially acknowledged your death and finished processing the paperwork, your most sensitive data is just "there," like so much zombie purchasing power.

More so than monitoring services or strong passwords, we all rely on ourselves to take action to combat identity theft—and you can only take action while you're still alive and kicking. And since very few of us know when that's going to change, it is crucial to get these matters squared away ahead of time.

Your anti-postmortem identity theft program will mostly take the form of a to-do list, since nothing can be done till . . . well, after the fact.

There are many different scams out there, ranging from the misappropriation of Social Security payments to the more old-fashioned practice of ghosting, whereby a person of approximately the same age assumes the identity of the deceased. Ghosting is less common than it used to be, but it does still happen.

Exhibit A: Don Draper, the brilliant, mercurial central character of AMC's hit show *Mad Men*. As Don's colleague Harry Crane says, "Draper? Who knows anything about that guy? No one's ever lifted that rock. He could be Batman for all we know."

Born Dick Whitman, the character we've come to know as Don Draper is the son of a young prostitute who dies in childbirth and an abusive alcoholic father who meets his maker compliments of a horse kick to the face when Draper/Whitman is ten.

From there, he is raised in a bordello, where . . . let's just say, bad things happened. To make a long backstory shorter, he drops out of high school, enlists in the army, and is sent to Korea, where he serves under Lieutenant Donald Francis Draper, an engineer assigned to build a field hospital with only Private Whitman to help. There is an accident, and Lieutenant Draper is killed, burned beyond recognition. Dick Whitman trades dog tags with the fallen officer. When he awakes in a hospital, he has become Draper. With the exception of a few scrapes with people who knew him as Dick—always dramatic moments on the show—Don Draper né Dick Whitman is a textbook example of a ghost.

Like Draper, most of the time a ghost is trying to avoid something—whether that is the law or gangsters, bad debt, or a bad marriage—by morphing into the persona of another who has no issues and a similar date of birth. This is one of the few crimes chosen by criminals who are trying to turn over a new leaf. It was common in the 1970s among a small demographic, the formerly radical members of violent student protest groups who had committed crimes—mostly bombings where no one got hurt—but no longer identified with the ideology that made them outlaws. Sometimes the ghost wasn't making an entirely clean break, something depicted well in Neil Gordon's *The Company You Keep*. During the Vietnam War era, draft dodgers fleeing to Canada or points elsewhere often adopted ghost identities that made it possible for them to live as citizens of whatever country they chose. And, of course, before the Jim Crow laws came to an end, light-skinned African Americans defined as Negro by the one-drop rule were very motivated to pass as Caucasian, and so ghosting became an option.

One peculiarity of this kind of identity theft is that it is easier to do for women, who often change their names when they get married. It's also easier for women to explain away long stretches of unemployment, attributing them to staying home to raise a family, even when they are secretly caused by a period of being dead, before being resurrected as someone else.

In keeping with the proliferation of possible crimes, there is no dearth of criminals out there who make a living in this deathly niche. They scan news the way cat burglars case homes, looking for death notices in the local paper, reading obituaries, even attending information-rich funerals (eulogies tend to contain a lot of personal information). Make no mistake about it: These scoundrels of the sweet hereafter can get a whole lot of shopping in before the three credit reporting agencies are notified of a person's demise. Doubtless, those same miscreants will almost certainly try to use your Social Security number to score a supersized tax refund (that is, if you're lucky enough to pass away during tax-filing season).

Ghostbook? Social Media and Death

According to a recent study by psychiatrist Elaine Kasket (yes, that's her real name), the ability to post photos and written testimonials to the deceased on social networking sites like Facebook can be important in helping friends deal with the loss. As long as those posts remain respectful, they could also help relatives better know the deceased and ease their process of mourning.

So far, the biggest actors in deciding these issues have been social networking sites themselves. Facebook allows family members to remove a deceased user's profile entirely, or place it in "memorial state," which removes status updates and restricts access to current friends, *Time* reports. Flickr continues preferences set by the user when he or she was alive, including barring anyone from seeing photos marked private.

Some of these policies make sense, but I foresee Solomonic problems. If a widow wants her dead husband's Facebook profile taken down, but his daughter wants it to remain active, how does Facebook decide? If a person has both a personal and a professional Facebook profile, might different rules of access apply for each?

How will they get the information needed to commit fraud? Sometimes the perpetrator is a family member, so they already have access. But more often, family members are distracted or distraught. There are visitors who come and go, unchecked, and of course the numerous demands of making final arrangements and dealing with matters of the estate can be distracting.

If there was a long illness, unsupervised healthcare workers may have had the run of the deceased's domicile—including unrestricted access to its owner's most sensitive information. If the wake was at the deceased's home, or people sat shiva there, still more vulnerabilities exist.

The opportunities for fraud abound. Funerals aren't only an opportunity for an identity thief to collect information about the deceased; they also provide criminals with a precise time to break into the decedent's home. But instead of grabbing the television or the silver (too easy to miss), they are there for an envelope containing a financial statement or a copy of a previous year's tax return. If a bad guy gets lucky, there is doubtless even more granular information or tasty transactional tidbits to be found in some homes—like credit cards, explanation of benefits statements, and account login information. From there, the race is on to apply for as much credit and buy as many pricy things for resale as possible before the money spigot runs dry.

> If you store sensitive information in your home— including tax returns, old financial statements, and identification documents— buy a safe.
>
> And use it properly.
>
> Seven percent of Americans don't lock their doors at night. Can you imagine how many don't lock safes inside their locked homes?

Why is this sort of crime possible?

Part of the problem lies with government agencies, which are famously slow to get the news of a person's demise. A recent audit of the Social Security Administration conducted by the Office of the Inspector General found that there were approximately 6.5 million Social Security numbers belonging to people aged 112 or older whose death information wasn't in the system. Of those numberholders, only thirteen people were still receiving payments. The rest of those Social Security numbers were associated with "numberholders who exceeded maximum reasonable life expectancies and were likely deceased." This uncertainty is an identity thief's bread and butter.

The fact that such an astronomical number of deaths have gone unrecorded in Numident (the SSA's numerical identification system), and thus are also missing in the Death Master File, leaves plenty of room for misconduct.

According to the audit report, the "SSA received 4,024 E-Verify inquiries using the SSNs of 3,873 numberholders born before June 16, 1901."

The report included a story about a scammer who managed to open bank accounts using zombie Social Security numbers. Those SSNs belonged to people who would have to be undead to open an account—and then only during evening hours. The Social Security numbers in question were issued to people born in 1869 and 1893, but, according to the Social Security Administration, they were still alive and well.

But there is another culprit, and if you get up right now and take a look in the mirror you can wave to him or her. It's you. We are all the ultimate guardians of our identity. For a complete DIY walk-through of steps you need to take and the documents required to close down a deceased person's identity, or to prepare your own estate so that family members or an executor can easily do it—all courtesy of the Identity Theft Resource Center—go to Appendices 3 through 5 in the back of the book.

While it's true that your liability is zero if you are a family member of a deceased person who becomes a victim of identity theft (the same goes for any legitimate debt of the dead, as long as there are no other names listed on the account in question), it's still no easy thing to go through. This is why it's important to be prepared. And it won't be easy to react when the trouble starts, so you might as well do it now.

12

Culture Eats Strategy

Business Considerations

Peter Drucker used to be a household name. These days, he doesn't get much play outside of management consultant circles, but in his heyday, Drucker was "the man who invented management." He had a great feel for what makes an organization hum, and when it comes to rethinking data security, that's precisely what we need at both the governmental and the enterprise levels.

It is a stretch to assume that our nation's leaders should set the tone for how things are done in the rest of the country, I suppose, but in an ideal world our leaders . . . well, they would lead. That has hardly been the case in the cyber realm.

Take, for instance, the lax approach to email security and data privacy that prevailed in the early days of the presidential campaigns of two leading candidates, Hillary Clinton and Jeb Bush. Early in the 2016 election cycle, Clinton's "emailgate" created a firestorm after it was revealed that the former secretary of state had used a home-brew email server instead of the policy-mandated servers of the State Department. The bigger affront was the assumption that her server was more secure than the government servers (though perhaps she was right: In the past few months, the State Department email system has been compromised by Russian hackers who don't seem to want to go away). Granted, the server in question was set up for President Bill Clinton, and it was protected by the Secret Service. But the nature of security is that it must operate with opacity, which means hiding things from the government.

> When it comes to data security, Rule Number One is that you don't talk about how you manage your data security. Rule Number Two is that you don't talk about the fact that you don't talk about how you manage your data security. This leaves a lot of room for fudging how you do data security.

So while the Clinton server may have been the most secure vehicle for communications in the country, there was no way for her boss (the president), reporters, or even lawmakers to confirm that. And when it comes to data security, no one gets a pass. This is where Secretary Clinton went wrong. She didn't set the bar; she crawled under it. She should have used the company email account, and she got called out. It was the right outcome.

Jeb Bush's "oops!" moment was different: He was careless. He took a laissez-faire approach to a problem that requires constant attention, imagination, quick reactions, and a kind of public-minded decision-making process that is constantly on the lookout for trouble and the best ways to avert it. In what Governor Bush billed as a show of transparency—an obvious dig at the famously secretive Clinton camp—he released more than 250,000 emails amassed over the course of his tenure as governor. Some of the messages released in Bush's transparency campaign contained the personally identifiable information of constituents—including Social Security numbers. While the move did not pose a national security risk, or rise anywhere near the level of Clinton's email problem, it demonstrated a poor understanding of data security and identity theft—or a nonexistent one.

The list of political leaders who just don't quite get the whole "data-security thing" is long. As mentioned in Chapter 3, South Carolina's governor Nikki Haley famously said that encryption was "hard" when accepting blame (or at least discussing blame) for a breach in her state that exposed the tax returns of 3.8 million tax-paying residents and 700,000 businesses, along with the Social Security numbers and bank accounts of not only the affected taxpayers, but nearly 2 million of their dependents. Or, for another quick example, remember the hacker who accessed Mitt Romney's personal email by guessing the name of his favorite pet? Bottom line, there is a tendency among our nation's leaders not to simply avoid the hard questions, but to remain blissfully, or even willfully, ignorant of how the most important data-security issues relate to the kinds of identity-related crimes that damage the lives of the people they are supposed to serve and represent—that is, until they find themselves on the wrong side of their ignorance and members of the news media take notice.

That same tendency is found in the business world. I would like to remind you of the response of Anthem's CEO regarding the breach involving the information of 80 million clients his company served. You may recall him touting the good news that no credit card information had been compromised. What had? Only full names, dates of birth, email addresses, and Social Security numbers. Either he didn't understand that this was far more dangerous, or, more likely, he didn't feel obligated to acknowledge it. At best, he was prepared to prioritize PR over the problem.

What we see over and over again is an institutional failure to grasp the way identity thieves work. There seems to be a general understanding that personal information needs to be protected, but somehow the idea that breaches are inevitable hasn't quite sunk in. Nor has the message that the bad guys out there are constantly hunting for vulnerabilities. (Remember, while a corporate cyberdefender must get everything right, a hacker only needs to find one vulnerability.) And it really doesn't matter if you are using a server set up for a former president or if you manage the

> **Say it with me: Data compromises are the third certainty in life.**

personally identifiable information of tens of millions of customers: there is no such thing as being beyond the reach—or notice—of hackers.

Drucker usually gets credit for the phrase, "Culture eats strategy for breakfast." These days, many companies have a strategy of some kind for protecting their data. But hackers have a culture of breaking down these defenses. That's bad news for your company's strategy.

Target was by no means the first major breach of a megacompany, but because it is an iconic retailer, the breach resonated with consumers, businesses, and lawmakers alike; fueled headlines for months; and resulted in a number of senior managers, including the CEO, walking the plank. One reason was that it happened during the holidays when the world was focused on shopping. The other reason was that the breach was simply so massive. It was disastrous for the company. It harmed the brand immeasurably. In fact, in many circles, the name Target is now synonymous with the word "breach."

Following news of the Target breach, first-quarter sales slid 16 percent from where they were during the same period the year before, and the company's stock lost more than 16 percent of its value. There were several factors that put a damper on earnings that year—including a total dud of an expansion into Canada that cost $941 million—but the damage caused by the breach cannot be underestimated.

A big part of Target's problem was that customers worried about shopping at the company. They didn't understand what had happened—not entirely—and they didn't want that dimly understood thing to happen again.

One of the biggest mistakes that organizations make after a breach is that they fail to educate their customers about what happened, what it may mean for them, and what they can do to minimize the damage. The drop-off in Target's earnings may have happened anyway, but they may have been avoided had Target's postbreach emphasis been less on risk assessment and messaging and more on mitigation through quick action and a customer-first response.

There were surveys that indicated that a lack of knowledge about what might be at stake—in other words, a public not terribly familiar with the uses of personal information by identity thieves—worked in Target's favor. There was one poll that found more than 60 percent of Target shoppers weren't concerned about data security. But as Sarah Palin once pointed out: Polls are for strippers and cross-country skiers.

For a time, the common wisdom was that a data breach in and of itself could undo years of brand equity, but with a parade of major breaches since, a different story has begun to emerge. Because breaches are becoming the new normal, companies will be judged in the future on how they prepared for the inevitable, and whether their incident response plans were urgent, transparent, and empathetic.

On May 28, 2014, the proxy adviser Institutional Shareholder Services (ISS) recommended that Target replace seven of its ten board members in order to put the company on a better path. According to the ISS statement, "The data breach revealed that the company was inadequately prepared for the significant risks of doing business in today's electronic commerce environment." It was a tense moment for that board, but they all survived. The shareholders were perhaps already of the mind that breaches were now part of the business landscape.

Target's interim chairperson wrote a spirited defense of the board, pointing out that before the November breach, Target had increased its information security team to three hundred employees, and that they were in the process of training more than 350,000 employees to better protect customer data. There was a lot in that defense. Target had a twenty-four-hour operations center constantly reviewing suspicious activity. They had invested a great deal in their security. And that was the argument. Essentially, "We tried." As we now know, it wasn't enough. The reason: human error. Yes, Target had contractors and employees manning the cyberbarricades. But when someone sounded the alarm—or rather when suspicious activity was detected and the FireEye monitoring technology sounded the bell—an utterly fallible human being overrode the warning system not once, but several times (as is often the case, there was a series of Paul Revere moments missed). The credit card data of millions of Target shoppers was leaked over a period of time that spanned several days, and it found its way onto the information black market.

The ISS recommendation to replace the board at Target came after the company had already taken steps to address its failure to imagine the scope of the pervasive cyberthreat. The CEO, Gregg Steinhafel, got a pair of cement shoes in early May. That came after the company announced a major hire. Bob DeRodes, who had previously worked for the Department of Homeland Security, would be the company's new chief information officer.

It was hard to know if the changes in leadership were more than symbolic. Right or wrong, the responsibility for this epic security fail was laid at the feet of the company's leader. It's hard to assign blame for Target's weak security, given that seemingly everyone is vulnerable to hacking, and *many* organizations—including Sony, Neiman Marcus, Home Depot, TD Bank, Michaels, JPMorgan Chase, and of course the White House—have already been breached. But when it came to notification, blame

> Speed, transparency, and empathy: the three requirements for a successful breach notification.

could be assigned. The response was not fast and it was not empathetic. There was no attempt to educate affected customers. The attitude was one of an embattled captain and his overwrought crew hoping to ride out a bad storm—and that reaction represented a major failure from the boardroom to the mailroom.

In the age of transparency and a twenty-four-hour news cycle that can start with a single outrageous tweet by a customer or client, there really is nowhere to run and nowhere to hide. That's been the flashlight-under-the-chin message that hackers have been trying to get out there for years. At first it seemed like boasting. Now it seems more like an understatement. And for anyone who has ever become the victim of an identity-related crime, the nowhere-to-hide message hits home with painful accuracy.

Target didn't get bad publicity simply because it got hacked. It got mangled by a lack of transparency, a failure to demonstrate urgency, and a response with limited empathy and maybe a little hubris.

After the smoke cleared, Target made a statement regarding data security: "Target was among the best-in-class within the retail industry," it said. Given the deplorable state of data security in retail, that wasn't saying much. Frankly, this makes you wonder whether anyone in retail security ever heard of cyber anything. More to the point, the reality is there is no such thing as a "best" when it comes to data security. Breaches are going to happen as surely as rain and sunshine. The new generation of hackers likes a challenge, and there seems to be nothing they can't crack if given the proper resources. With enough computing power and a little dumb luck, or, more to the point, with a properly worded email to an underinformed employee (or vendor employee)—one who has never had a training session about data security and best practices—there is no system online that cannot be compromised and exploited.

Target's problem was a failure in vision—and that's why it's right that the CEO took a walk. It's one thing to talk about your "guests" in glittering generalities, but if there is nothing backing it up, you're lost. Companies that want to survive the breaches that are more and more a certainty need to cultivate and nurture a strong culture of data-security awareness. A good host makes sure their guests don't die of identity-theft-fueled heart attacks. A guest is supposed to have a good experience. Or at least not come out feeling ill-used or abused or swindled. As breaches become a reality of doing business, it's all about reaction. What do you do when your customer's information has been breached? Everyone from the ground crew to the CEO needs to know. Breach response must be planned. It must be discussed. It must be drilled. It needs to become second nature so that when the dark day of a data breach arrives, the notification and resolution process is pure muscle memory. Data security must become a part of a company's culture, just like employee benefits and legal affairs.

When culture takes a backseat to insincere remorse dispensed by publicity departments charged with moving product and "growing the brand" rather than saving it from ignominy, you are going to need much more than a voucher for identity theft monitoring and a 10 percent off sale to attract customers. In March 2015, Target announced that it would be eliminating 1,700 jobs and another 1,400 would go unfilled. They would use the money saved to bolster online sales and create new brick-and-mortar strategies. That announcement followed the shuttering of 133 stores in Canada that were opened after the breach, and the pink-slipping of 550 positions at its Twin Cities headquarters a month earlier. Was this all because of the breach? That's doubtful, but the data breach was a big disadvantage in a highly competitive marketplace—the kind of problem Target could ill afford. With the absence of similar strategies being deployed at other big-box stores, the breach certainly looks like it had an impact.

In a corporate culture that assumes and prepares for the worst-case data-security scenarios, and puts the emphasis on urgency,

---

Used Against You in a Court of Law . . .

Coming to a jurisdiction near you: Companies that harvest private information may very well be called to testify in lawsuits based on the data they hold. Telegraphing what will doubtless become a future strategy, a personal injury claim represented by McLeod Law in Calgary, Canada, included evidence culled from Fitbit data to prove that a client was still suffering four years after an accident.

---

transparency, and empathy, the true risk of a breach—massive loss of customer loyalty—can be contained and perhaps reversed. Putting the pitfalls of the inevitable into human terms is how you build and sustain brand equity.

The Sony breach highlights the culture problem. Sony's former head Amy Pascal knows this only too well—it cost her a job. She got caught participating in a racially tinged email thread about President Obama's taste in movies and expressing herself in disrespectful terms while talking about celebrities attached to Sony projects, including Kevin Hart, Joel McHale, and megastar Angelina Jolie, the latter being dissed as "a minimally talented spoiled brat" by producer Scott Rudin in a back-and-forth slapfest with the Sony Pictures cochair.

There is no way to intelligently downplay the Sony hack. It doesn't matter that it was likely perpetrated by a nation state. What matters is the fact that it was not anticipated. Like most large companies that suffer a breach, Sony Pictures will weather this storm, but it's taken a beating. In the best-case scenario the fallout from a breach represents a huge opportunity cost. I suppose on some level there is a bit of irony in the fact that a motion picture studio is guilty of such a colossal failure of the imagination. The assumption should have been that all work product— including email, scripts, and finished movies—were neither secure nor beyond the reach of a motivated attacker.

The amount of information that was captured in the Sony hack was pure cyber box office. Scripts were leaked, and unreleased movies found their way to pirate sites. Social Security numbers of past and present employees—47,000 of them—were flung into the cybersphere. Payouts to Sylvester Stallone, Judd Apatow, and other celebrities were made public. Thousands of controversial emails were left to dangle for all the world to see. And while the financial damage was no doubt serious, the compromise also raised grave concerns about the future of doing business in the age of the superhack. It doesn't matter if you run a mom-and-pop shop or a multinational giant like Sony, Anthem, or Target—your future is on the line if you don't breach-proof your business.

That doesn't mean preventing your company from being breached, because that's impossible. The FBI said that there weren't many companies—possibly as few as 10 percent—that could have prevented an attack like the one that targeted Sony. There would have been a better outcome if there had been better data-security protocols in place. But those protocols would have had to include rules about what you can and can't say in an email. It would have had to speak to the way you handle the files of former employees (When should they be destroyed? Do they need to live online? Have they been encrypted?), and it would need to consider ways to limit the use of proprietary data—including product—when stolen. Throwing your hands in the air and pointing to the impossibility of the situation when saddled with an unprecedented event is a slippery slope that almost assuredly ends with both horse and rider in a ditch.

The teachable moment in the Sony Pictures breach was that security has to be practiced at the individual level and the enterprise level. It means assuming that your email may someday become viewable by the entire world. It means assuming your protections will fail, and constantly

> A data breach is potentially an extinction-level event for a company.

revising your defenses with new fail-safe features. Security has to be sewn into the very fabric of daily life at the office; it must be part of an enterprise's corporate culture.

You are the sum total of your hires, and a big breach puts the spotlight on the people who, at least in the public's eyes, should have done a better job. That means everyone is on the spot—but particularly the board of directors and the people they chose to place in the C suite. Leaders lead. It sounds silly, but it means that key players in any organization need to acquire and demonstrate a level of sophistication, nuance, sensitivity, and respect when communicating internally, whether or not those communications involve high-profile people—like A-list celebrities, for example. Given the fact that a breach is inevitable, you should assume it will happen.

People will talk, and when status or a higher salary is on the line, it will get personal. The *All About Eve* tendency to supplant, crush, or conquer will never be eradicated from corporate life. That said, if your employees understand the costs of getting caught *not* being a team player, you may head off the worst kinds of communication—the stuff of maximum new media entertainment value in the wake of a breach. There's an upside to modeling a high-road approach to work, since a lack of respect tolerated in emails almost always translates into bad morale. And a weak esprit de corps can very easily become manifest in a company's approach to data security—since, really, who cares if the personally identifiable information of my colleagues gets stolen?

If there's no guarantee your email won't at some point be leaked, the solution cannot be Orwellian. No company would come out looking clean if all

> Assume you're going to be hacked, and revealed as an imperfect human being, like everyone else. And be good. Or, at the very least, consider picking up the phone when you have something to say that you wouldn't want broadcast on the evening news.

their email were exposed. Is it an overreach to ask employees to write all their correspondence in a *Brady Bunch* mode? Of course it is.

The key may be to emphasize ownership among a company's staff—at least in the figurative sense. In the Sony Pictures breach, films were stolen, as were countless other assets, including scripts, budgets, and even intimate details of contract negotiations. Ownership is a state of mind that requires upkeep and vigilance to protect what's yours, and it can start with a simple statement such as, "This is my area. I'm in charge of X." Ownership creates security. Ultimately, this starts with corporate leadership, since fostering a sense of ownership among employees is a trickle-down process.

A strong corporate culture is a work in progress, constantly evolving. It stays ahead of the curve because it never stops applying the processes that make it successful—the consequence of clear leadership and a culture where employees feel invested in their work is that they take ownership of the tasks assigned to them. Something like the Sony hack—where the enemy is well armed, fully weaponized, and in war mode—may not be avoidable, but a state of readiness, predicated by a healthy corporate culture that puts security first, is the only way such an attack can be properly contained and managed.

> Data breaches didn't exist when the German poet Rainer Maria Rilke wrote, "for here there is no place that does not see you. You must change your life," but that doesn't matter. It's particularly sound advice today.

A study released by the Ponemon Institute last year found that the average cost of an enterprise-level breach in 2013 was $3.5 million, and the most recent figure is $3.8 million. If you need something concrete to believe that data breaches can be an extinction-level event for many companies, a figure like that should do the trick. But if you approach data security in a more holistic way, the threat of breaches can actually be a moneymaker.

While it should be clear that the time to change the way businesses approach data security was the day before yesterday, what may not be as obvious is the fact that the framework for a solution already exists. It was first discussed in the 1990s, in a slightly different guise, by Ontario's now-former information and privacy commissioner Ann Cavoukian. She is the progenitor of "privacy by design."

At the very beginning of privacy's emergence as a profit center, when companies began mining personal data and repackaging it to retailers, websites, advertisers, and marketing companies, Cavoukian discerned a limit to what consumers would tolerate; they would quickly understand that "free" services were merely a way to separate them from their personal information for use in marketing campaigns aimed right back at them. She also rightly saw that companies that offered clients options would become de rigueur, a foresight that even privacy-hostile Facebook had to

---

The Big Idea: Privacy by Design

Privacy by design is a marketing tactic whose time has come. It gets around the question, "How safe will my personal information be with your organization?" by making privacy and data security a marketing point. Increasingly, consumers know that whenever something's free, their information is the product—sold to a third party. More and more people are paying greater attention to the way a company talks about privacy and data security.

As companies are starting to discover, the new market demand will give rise to well-presented privacy-by-design marketing plans that may be able to convert curious window-shoppers into customers. Of course, if you talk about privacy and data security in a way that suggests you might not really know what you're talking about (for instance, by touting the use of password protection and "state-of-the-art storage"), it could have the opposite effect.

eventually make real, after denying there was such a thing as privacy for some time. When Facebook users got privacy toggles, it was clear the privacy-by-design idea had legs.

Twenty years later, privacy by design has become a term of art used in marketing meetings, and while not everyone sees the matter in precisely the same way, a company's approach to the issue of consumer privacy is now something that gets figured out in the planning process and not just tacked on after the fact. That's what the market wants.

Taking a page out of Cavoukian's playbook, I floated the idea of security by design, which started getting marketed in earnest after the megabreaches of the past couple of years.

Here are Cavoukian's seven principles of privacy by design, which can easily be adapted for the security-by-design concept:

1. Be proactive, not reactive; focus on preventative, not remedial. The company "does not wait for privacy risks to materialize, nor does it offer remedies for resolving privacy infractions once they have occurred—it aims to prevent them from occurring." Security by design would focus on eliminating the risks associated with storing third-party information.
2. Privacy should be the default setting. "If an individual does nothing, their privacy still remains intact. No action is required" on the part of the individual to protect his or her privacy. It is built into the system. Ditto with security by design: Consumers should not have to worry about the security of their data when they make a transaction.
3. Privacy should be embedded into the design and architecture of IT systems and business practices, "not bolted on as an add-on." Security must be part of the design process, as well.

4. A positive-sum, not zero-sum, approach avoids "false dichotomies, such as privacy vs. security, demonstrating that it is possible to have both."

5. End-to-end security is "embedded into the system prior to the first element of information being collected, and extends throughout the entire lifecycle of the data involved, from start to finish. This ensures that at the end of the process, all data are securely destroyed, in a timely fashion." This point would remain virtually unchanged from Cavoukian's original concept.

6. Visibility/invisibility and transparency/opacity: The privacy-by-design model says that companies need to tell consumers exactly what they are going to do with the information they collect. While this works for privacy by design, it would put a giant target, if you'll excuse the pun, on a company that touts its security. There's no greater magnet for a hacker than a good challenge. Security by design requires invisibility and opacity.

7. Respect for the consumer: As with privacy by design, security by design "requires architects and operators to keep the interests of the individual uppermost by offering such measures as strong privacy defaults, appropriate notice and empowering user-friendly options."

Security by design speaks to the culture question. It's not lip service. You can't say you're doing security by design and leave it at that. Hackers will continue to get better at hacking, just as companies will continue to get better at fighting them off. That's part of the design. Both large- and small-business owners still need to be prepared for a breach and its aftermath.

13

The Three Ms for Companies

You Must Build It Because They Will Come

The Three Ms are a bit different when you start thinking about how you might implement them to protect not just yourself, but a larger group that may contain either identity theft victims or unwitting coconspirators, also known as employees, who unwittingly make a database compromise possible.

If you think the cost-benefit ratio is off, consider that the consolidated worldwide average cost of a breach to a company is $154 per record, according to the Ponemon Institute's 2015 Global Cost of Data Breach study. As mentioned in Chapter 12, Ponemon found that the average cost of a breach to a company reached $3.8 million (before considering things like loss of reputation, business partners, and consumers), representing a 23 percent increase over the previous year.

On April 1, 2015, ThirdCertainty, an online thought leadership publication sponsored by my company, IDT911, featured an article that highlighted the results of a recent survey of more than eight hundred technology officials—representing American and European companies and organizations employing at least five hundred people—performed by the CyberEdge Group, a Maryland-based research and marketing consultant for high-tech vendors and service providers. Respondents answered twenty-seven questions. Key findings were that 61 percent of respondents expect to raise their IT budgets this year, while 52 percent expect to be successfully attacked by hackers before December 31. With cyberattacks geometrically increasing by the day, organizations are planning to spend more this year, with an average of 6–10 percent of their IT budgets devoted to cybersecurity. Some 20 percent of them will be spending more than 16 percent.

CyberEdge CEO Steve Piper said that he believes the findings should inspire organizations to address the following questions:

- Is there a security technology we have overlooked?
- Have we made enough investment in employee security-awareness training?
- Do we have the ability to decrypt Secure Sockets Layer (SSL) traffic to find hidden threats?
- Are we doing the right things to reduce our attackable surface?
- Are we properly monitoring privileged user accounts?

These are certainly crucial questions because seven in ten respondents admitted their networks had been breached. Of the 70 percent who had been breached, over 20 percent had been breached at least six times.

The causes of the breaches: Employees (human error—respondents singled out low security awareness among employees) and insufficient funds being budgeted.

Whose fault is that? Before you answer, take a moment to reflect upon this: For the second year in a row, mobile devices—smartphones and tablets—were considered key points of IT vulnerability. (Nearly 60 percent said they saw an increase in mobile device threats in the past twelve months.)

So what are they going to do about it? Before you answer *that*, read the following discomfiting results from a recent Ponemon

Institute study of four hundred megaorganizations commissioned by IBM: Sixty-seven percent of the very big organizations that were surveyed (apparently, when it comes to system security, they aren't too big to fail) allow their employees to download unverified personal apps on their workplace devices, the same phones and tablets that can also access highly confidential customer records and customer data. And this irresponsible attitude extends far beyond the workplace.

According to the *VentureBeat* article by Subbu Sthanu of IBM that discusses the IBM/Ponemon study, 50 percent of companies dedicate none of their budget to securing the mobile apps they build for customers, who often—without a moment's hesitation—upload of their most confidential billing, personal, and business data. And you want to know why all companies are at risk?

So, in the face of such a grim survey, what's an enterprise to do? Whatever their decision, it best be

- properly funded—this is not the area to be penny-wise and pound-foolish;
- comprehensive—employees must be continuously trained in methods designed to eliminate them as the weakest link; and
- focused—isolate areas of perceived (or future) weakness and fix them.

Here, then, are some basic guidelines for an enterprise version of the Three Ms that should be guiding principles for all organizations.

Minimize Your Risk of Exposure

The most important step you can take is to be proactive about your own security, rather than trying to do a work-around, or a complete overhaul, in the event your organization becomes a breach statistic.

- **Do a risk assessment.** You need to develop and implement an enterprise-wide process to identify and assess threats, vulnerabilities, attacks, probabilities of occurrence, and outcomes. If you are a retailer, you need to look beyond the point-of-sale environment.

- **When you design your systems, always begin with the end in mind—and the end must always be security.** Make sure that you adopt a standards-based security architecture that is integrated into all technology processes.

- **Employee security-awareness training is as essential as the air we breathe.** Your employees represent a key security defense. They are often a hacker's first point of attack (think spearphishing, easily decipherable passwords, mindlessly misplaced cell phones and laptops, and improperly secured devices that access your secure systems). You can achieve effective employee awareness and understanding through comprehensive security training and ongoing security-related communications, employee certifications of compliance, self-assessments, audits, and monitoring. It is imperative that they clearly understand the risks to your organization (and therefore to their jobs) if they become the object of a hacker's attention.

- **Your security must be layered.** Like very tall, electrified fences and deadbolts on your doors, multiple layers of security can slow down cyberthieves as well as limit what they can access and pilfer in a single attack. Adopt a "minimum necessary access" policy. Allow users (and their devices) only what they need to perform their required tasks. Update access rights in response to personnel or system changes. Never permit multiple employees (or department members) to share a password, assign each a discrete password, and never allow them to share passwords among various systems.

- **Your systems should always be asking, "Do I know you?"** Use two-factor authentication on everything you can and require that your employees do as well. Protect the confidentiality of data and create individual accountability for actions performed on your system by verifying the unique identity of each system user. Require two or more shared secret identity credentials everywhere you can, especially for private financial and healthcare information: Something the user knows, something the user has, or something the user is.

- **Your systems must be segregated.** Segregate your financial, security, and customer and employee data-storage systems from each other as well as from the systems and data used for routine operations management (think Target).

- **CYA if you allow BYOD ("Bring Your Own Device").** If you permit employees or outside contractors to access your secure systems with their portable electronic devices (i.e., cell phones, tablets, or laptops), establish stringent security protocols that all devices must meet (or have your own information security experts install appropriate software on them) before they are allowed to connect to your secure systems. Adopt a zero-tolerance policy toward anyone who fails to adhere to your policies.

- **Never underestimate the importance of physical security.** Identify those areas of your business where you store your most sensitive information and highest-value assets. Implement meaningful preventative and detection controls where necessary to protect against physical penetration by malicious or unauthorized people, damage from environmental contaminants, and unauthorized electronic intrusion.

- **Develop proper file retention and destruction policies.** Limit your legal liability and breach exposures by developing appropriate retention requirements for both hard copy and electronic files, and employing secure destruction practices for electronic data, physical files (think shredding), and any hardware that either you are no longer required to keep or has become obsolete.

- **You should never hesitate to consult outside, trusted experts.** Have regular third-party security assessments and penetration testing. Never rely solely on your internal security assets or processes.

Monitor Your Security

Don't rely on any system or software you set up last year to be relevant next year. On an ongoing basis, make sure that you do the following:

- **Monitor information security controls.** Routinely monitor your systems to confirm and reconfirm that the data-security protocols you've put in place are sufficiently robust to effectively shield your most precious assets. Periodically test them to ensure their ongoing effectiveness is where you need it to be. Whether you do this internally or engage a trusted third party as an outside observer, it is critical for you to be aware of any degradation in your security protocols before cyberthieves take advantage of any vulnerability. As a defender, you need to have everything working correctly. An intruder need only find one crack. And when monitoring and testing confirms that you are standing strong and getting stronger, don't forget to appropriately recognize your information security team for making this happen.

- **Perform vulnerability scans, penetration testing, configuration analysis, and social engineering testing.** Use a reputable outside firm to perform periodic tests of your network to ensure that no unauthorized user can gain access. If a vulnerability is detected, fix the problem immediately. Today's necessary best practices are comprehensive, and include vulnerability assessments to identify where you have security gaps, configuration analysis that benchmarks your security settings to those required to thwart the latest exploits, as well as penetration testing of your network and social engineering testing of your employees' ability to resist intruders and phishing attacks that allow hackers to gain access. If you find any holes, fix the problem immediately.

- **Monitor for intrusion.** It is as mission critical to data security to continuously monitor your electronic security perimeter and quickly alert information security personnel when there is an intrusion as it is to monitor and alert your physical security personnel in the event someone were to break into your offices.

- **Manage an information security program.** Delegate the authority to direct your information security program to someone with the right skills and proven talents, and give them the time and space to do whatever they need to make it work the way it should. It is immaterial whether you call them your compliance officer, information security officer, or CISO. What matters is that you centralize responsibility for managing your data security, devote full-time employees to it, and emphasize that you expect your designee to keep you personally informed. Also make sure that you keep your board informed.

Being secure is a daily responsibility—you are never finished. Even though you may be secure at the moment, you cannot rest on your laurels—cyberthieves certainly don't. Proper cybersecurity demands a programmatic strategy, discipline, and continuous testing to ensure that your employees are adhering to your tactical plans. It is no different from your approach to growing your business.

If you don't have someone with the necessary skillset, or can't afford to hire someone full time for this position, consider "virtual CISO" or "fractional CISO" services that are offered by trusted third-party service providers. Bottom line: Centralizing and focusing this security function is more important than who does the work.

- **Establish a patch management program.** Invest to establish a patch-management program that is overseen by a responsible person who provides you with periodic reports on the program's effectiveness and monitors and installs all security updates for software and operating systems in a timely fashion (think Premera) on all devices, even those brought in by your employees.

- **Require contracts with vendors and service providers.** Think of your vendors and third-party service providers—particularly those from whom you obtain hosted data or cloud-computing services—as you would your own employees. (Heaven knows the regulators and class-action attorneys are beginning to think of them that way.)

Once your customer and employee data is in their care and custody, it is outside of your direct control, and the best you can hope for is that they live up to the contractual commitments they have made to protect it. Before signing any contract put forth by a vendor or service provider, always read the fine print very carefully to make sure you understand where they claim their responsibilities end and yours begin.

Make sure that you contractually demand data protections that are equal to or better than yours in-house, that your contracts require you be notified immediately if your data suffers a breach, and that you take all necessary steps to verify the vendor's security capabilities before you begin doing business with them. Always question, and only trust after you have verified. And never forget that each contract renewal gives you the same opportunity.

Manage the Damage

Even if they haven't yet, it is highly likely that every organization will experience some sort of breach in the coming years. So don't solely rely on best practices to prevent future problems. Recognize that cyberattacks are more frequent, diverse, and persistent than ever before and they have the potential to disrupt your business, damage your firm's reputation, and possibly create a near extinction-level event for you.

- **First responders.** You would be well advised to invest in an incident response capability that rapidly detects cyberattacks, minimizes related loss and destruction, mitigates the weaknesses that were exploited, restores IT services, addresses any required notifications and reports in the case of a data breach, and responds urgently, transparently, and empathetically to all those exposed.

Designate an incident response team within your organization comprised of employees with IT, media, crisis-management, and people skills. Have them create an incident response program that games a number of scenarios and plans your responses. Update the plan in response to changes in your business, IT systems, and new cybercrime threats.

- **Cyber insurance.** Use insurance coverage as an effective method to transfer cybercrime risks to insurance carriers. Coverage is increasingly available to cover risks from security breaches or denial-of-service attacks. Several insurance companies offer e-commerce insurance packages that can reimburse companies for losses from fraud, privacy breaches, system downtime, or incident response. When evaluating the need for insurance to cover information security threats, the *U.S. FFIEC Information Security IT Examination Handbook* outlines the following points for enterprises:

  1. Insurance is not a substitute for an effective security program.
  2. Traditional fidelity bond coverage may not protect from losses related to security intrusions.
  3. Availability, cost, and covered risks vary by insurance company. Carefully evaluate the extent and availability of coverage in relation to the specific risks you are seeking to mitigate.

- **Breach notification.** Make sure that your incident response plan (and your insurance coverage) covers all the costs of a data breach—like the expense of notifying those customers and employees whose data was exposed—and ensure that the plan will help you and your customers navigate the aftermath. Do not be penny-wise and pound-foolish. The few bucks you save today might well cost you millions (you read that right—millions) in the future.

- **Incident reporting.** Make sure you understand what, if any, time-sensitive reporting requirements are mandated after a breach in order to both comply with legal requirements and maintain your coverage. Breach notification laws exist in forty-seven states, the District of Columbia, Guam, Puerto Rico, and the Virgin Islands. Notification time frames, and the parties that must be notified, vary by state. Federal laws such as the Health Insurance Portability and Accountability Act (HIPAA), Children's Online Privacy Protection (COPPA), and the Gramm-Leach-Bliley Act also may apply, and failure to comply can lead to regulatory penalties, reputational damage, and loss of business. Notification laws are manageable with the right guidance. If you are uncertain about any aspect of the process, engage a proven third-party service provider to advise and guide you.

- **Reputation management.** Decide how you will deal with any postbreach media: Will you designate someone internally to be your company's public face, or will you hire an outside organization to do it for you? (And, if so, who might you want to hire?)

    Have a plan in place for how you will deal with postbreach phone calls from affected employees or customers.

    Decide what you will do for those individuals affected by the breach. Though it's now standard to offer one-size-fits-all credit monitoring regardless of the type of breach, that often isn't nearly enough for those who have been either exposed or victimized. You should contract with an identity theft services provider to guide victims through the reporting and resolution process, and have the work done for them.

The dangers you face from a data breach often go far beyond penalties, fines, regulatory interactions, and litigation. Depending on the public's perception of the urgency, empathy, and transparency you demonstrate, you could face a devastating loss of trust by business partners, consumers, and employees alike.

To even begin to prevent that kind of damage, you must be as protective of the customer and employee data you gather and store as you are with your own trade secrets or intellectual property.

14

The Highest Law

At his best, man is the noblest of all animals; separated
from law and justice he is the worst.

—ARISTOTLE

This almost 2,500-year-old piece of wisdom by Aristotle provides
an amazingly accurate description of where we find ourselves with
regard to data-breach and cybersecurity legislation. One thing
that has become painfully obvious over the past few years is that
corporations and organizations will generally tiptoe back and
forth over the line between right and wrong, especially when it
comes to protecting the personally identifiable information of the
people with whom they do business. They strive to obey the law,
but always just barely.

When Cicero said, "The safety of the people shall be the highest law," he didn't know about the U.S. Congress. Without pointing fingers, I will say that our representatives in Washington do
not always fight for what's right in the realm of data security. In
fact, more often than not, it seems that they carry the spit buck-
ets for big businesses that view data security as just another costly
compliance "nightmare," along the lines of the Dodd-Frank Wall
Street Reform and Consumer Protection Act, which costs the
banking industry around $34 billion annually.

But as with Dodd-Frank, one CEO's nightmare is an entire population's job-killing recession. Now, you may be disappointed to

hear this if you're a true believer in our great democratic experiment, but many lawmakers aren't the consumer's best friends. Alabama Republican Spencer Bachus, former chairman of the House banking committee, famously (or perhaps infamously) said that Congress and federal regulators should take their orders from banks. Remember the quote? "In Washington, the view is that the banks are to be regulated, and my view is that Washington and the regulators are there to serve the banks." That's what Bachus told the *Birmingham News*. Bachus eventually decided to pursue a new line of work, but there are a whole lot more just like him, doing the Washington two-step.

The first order of business, then, is to measure the value of a law not by how much it might cost a company to implement, but by its costs and benefits to the actual consumers who drive the economy. By that measure, Dodd-Frank was worth it (Mitch McConnell's protestations notwithstanding). And by that measure, we will have to create laws about data security and data-breach notification that are worth it.

There is a long history of bills seeking to regulate both data privacy and cybersecurity that never survived a committee vote, much less made it through either house of Congress. Some failed because authors or cosponsors didn't grasp the enormity of the problem. Some failed because they didn't manifest the necessary gravitas to overcome opposition from businesses and consumers alike. Others attempted to differentiate privacy and data security as separate line items, when in reality they are more like the strands of the double helix that comprises DNA, linked again and again at every turn.

These legislative false starts include a few notable attempts in 2005, 2007, and 2009. The last of these squeezed through the Senate Judiciary Committee only to get annihilated by special interests, mainly corporations. So, it died long before a vote could be scheduled in the full Senate. Since then, there have been bills that tried to criminalize the failure to disclose breaches, and others that attempted to force companies to go public with the details of a breach within forty-eight hours of its discovery. President Obama tried his hand at a law that would cut through the morass—it was an also-ran. The Cybersecurity Act of 2012 most likely got killed more or less on the basis of what it would cost to implement, though opponents cited government regulation and potential for businesses to spy on consumers as reasons for their opposition. Compliance is never a cheap date.

Without exception, attempts thus far at an enforceable federal standard have fallen well short of the protections offered in the most privacy-forward states, and they've died for reasons good, bad, and ugly. Voting for a weak federal law that replaces stronger state laws will get you in trouble with constituents, while voting for legislation that will cost companies a lot on the compliance side is a guaranteed way to have empty war chests come election time.

A couple of years ago, the Health Insurance Portability and Accountability Act (HIPAA) and more recent amendments to the law in the Health Information Technology for Economic and Clinical Health Act (HITECH)—the laws that establish regulatory frameworks to govern the handling of sensitive health-related data or PHI—arguably made our electronic medical records a lot safer. As welcome as the change was, we need to go further. Privacy and data security are tightly connected when it comes to lawmaking, and the focus should be on deciding which data companies should be permitted to collect, and how to keep that data safe. For sure, it's time for a federal law requiring encryption of *any* database that contains personally identifiable information, but while we're at it, let's update the definitions of PII.

As the epic data-protection fails of the health industry have demonstrated, encryption is an indispensable tool for securing electronically stored and transmitted protected health information (PHI). And, as such, this data-security protocol is the best bet for keeping patient privacy intact. The relationship between the two issues is so fundamental, in fact, that even though encryption isn't strictly required by HIPAA and HITECH, it is, as a practical matter, impossible to comply with HIPAA regulations *without* using it.

Without encryption, there really is no effective way to keep electronic patient data secure. When you consider the alternatives to encryption, and how damaging those alternatives are to patient and healthcare provider alike, the insanity of *not* encrypting should be apparent. However, insanely enough, unencrypted medical records are still leaked *all the time*. A case in point: the Health and Human Services' "wall of shame." It's a list posted by the HHS secretary of breaches involving unsecured protected health information that affected five hundred individuals or more. That list contains an embarrassing number of laptops that were lost or stolen with unencrypted PHI on their hard drives. And every one of those laptops came from someone who should have known better—but who, nevertheless, chose to put their patients at risk. (Doesn't the Hippocratic oath say, *Primum non nocere*—"First, do no harm"?) Then, of course, there are all those breaches involving insiders pilfering files, hackers piercing inadequately secured databases, and the newest threat to medical data security—mobile devices. But no law is better than a good criminal. As discussed previously, this was never more evident than in the cases of the insurance giants Anthem and Premera.

In terms of size and scope, the Anthem breach was one of the worst in history. Nearly every meaningful piece of the PII of 78.8 million adults and children—save their medical information—was exposed to hackers: names, physical addresses, dates of birth, email addresses, phone numbers, medical IDs, employment information, and Social Security numbers. Not to be outdone, a few weeks later, Premera announced its breach, which exposed every shred of PII and PHI it had on some 11 million adults and children through an attack on the IT side. Adding insult to injury, shortly before the Premera breach, a security audit carried out by the Office of Personnel Management (OPM), which has a contract with the insurer, identified critical security patches that hadn't been applied in a timely manner. So, here we are, once again proving the extremely depressing fact that for around 90 million Americans, though they may have done everything right to protect their identities at a personal level, the folks they looked to as guardians of their health and protectors of their patient privacy still failed them. And now they will be forced to keep looking over their shoulders for the rest of their (and their children's) lives.

The post-Snowden outcry over NSA surveillance put encryption and the fragility of privacy back in the spotlight. Revelations of the NSA's spying on phone calls, email, and other Internet traffic had an upside: It jolted Americans into realizing their private correspondence might not be so private after all—and, perhaps, caused us to reflect on the value of privacy and the ways data security can best protect it.

That said, with each passing brand-name megabreach—whether we talk about Premera, Home Depot, Target, JPMorgan Chase, or Anthem—it becomes ever more urgent for government and industry to communicate, cooperate, and collaborate on the most effective ways to protect consumers.

As I hope has become evident here, not all laws are created equal, and there are few better examples of this homespun truth than a recent would-be federal law: the Data Security and Breach Notification Act of 2015. Unfortunately, it isn't very successful in terms of battling the problem. But perhaps the failure is instructive: The bill illustrates what we need to look for in whatever eventually becomes the law of the land regarding privacy and data security.

According to public record, the Data Security and Breach Notification Act of 2015 "aims to tackle the nation's growing data security threats and challenges." So far, so good. The bill was authored by full committee, with Energy and Commerce Committee vice chair Marsha Blackburn (R-TN) and Rep. Peter Welch

(D-VT) making it a bipartisan effort. The goal: to implement "a comprehensive plan to help safeguard sensitive consumer information and shield Americans from the harmful consequences of cyber attacks."

The problem with this proposal is not that it tries to be all things, but rather that it doesn't try to be enough—and, compounding that shortcoming, there are far more effective laws already on the books in several states. That immediately becomes an issue, since they could be preempted if the bill were to pass. And if that wasn't bad enough, the proposed bill could also supersede stronger rules already promulgated by the FCC with regard to telephone, broadband Internet, cable, and satellite user information.

While undermining better laws is bad, worse is the way the Data Security and Breach Notification Act of 2015 underscores a continuing failure of our leaders to fully understand the nature of the problems we face in this arena.

In a widely publicized survey conducted by the Pew Research Center, "91% of adults in the survey 'agree' or 'strongly agree' that consumers have lost control over how personal information is collected and used by companies." We need a strong federal law, but any proposed bill that threatens to weaken existing laws must always be challenged quickly and without equivocation.

Senior policy counsel at New America's Open Technology Institute Laura Moy did just that, eloquently outlining the problems this bill could create in testimony before the House of Representatives.

In a wide-ranging discussion of the major concerns raised by the bill, Moy pointed out some of the laws that could be preempted. One was California's Song-Beverly Credit Card Act, which made it illegal to record a credit card holder's personal identification information during a transaction. Another law in Connecticut outlawing the public posting of any individual's Social Security number was also named. Both state laws represent solid advances in the realm of data security, and both might be preempted if the bill moving through Congress is enacted.

And here's the really bad news: They would be two of the *less* alarming casualties.

The problem, in the broadest of terms, is a failure of definitions. The proposed bill has made a crucial error by trying to separate consumer privacy and personal information security, when in reality the boundaries between the two are porous at best. It's a problem because the narrow legal definitions of each term could weaken or even eliminate protections for the many kinds of information that fall outside the bill's purview. Identity thieves, inevitably, will find ways to deploy this information for their profit—and consumers won't have any recourse to stop them.

As Moy argued during her testimony, "Many laws that protect consumers' personal information [can] be thought of simultaneously in terms of both privacy and security." I will go one step further and say that I do not believe it is possible to discuss data security until we have a worst-case-scenario definition of what constitutes personally identifiable information in the eyes of an identity thief.

To give an example of the kinds of preemption that are possible here, Florida's privacy law includes the consumer's email address and username-password combination in its definition of personal information, the logic being that consumers use the same combination for many different login pages, including financial accounts. Seven states currently mandate the same standard—California, Missouri, New Hampshire, North Dakota, Texas, Florida, and Virginia—and on July 1, 2015, Hawaii and Wyoming joined them. Under the currently proposed bill, these laws will be preempted, and usernames and passwords will be unprotected by law. Meanwhile, these kinds of information continue to be highly exploitable data points in an identity thief's toolkit.

In addition to the exemption of breaches that "only" include email addresses or user login details, the bill is unclear about the personal information of customers subscribing to telecom-munications, cable, and satellite services, which hinge on a trigger of "authorized access" that, Moy believes, may super-sede important protections. Most alarming is the prospect of less robust notifications regarding compromised customer proprietary network information (CPNI), which includes texts, phone calls, your location when you made each phone call, your location when you *didn't* make a phone call, and the loca-tions of all your network-connected devices. All this informa-tion could be breached, and the Data Security and Breach Notification Act of 2015 says you don't need to know about it. The same goes for what you watch on television, including any items you may have purchased on pay-per-view. All of it could be out there, open to public perusal. No one is required to tell you if this happens.

Critics have noted that there is no reference to protected health information in the bill, which suggests that either Congress does not understand identity theft, or it is too politicized to care. Ei-ther way, it's actually a bit of good news that PHI has been entirely carved out here. With a few notable preemptions of existing state law affecting over-the-counter purchases and other health-related items, most forms of PHI would still be covered by the notifica-tion requirements of the HIPAA/HITECH Act.

According to the narrow logic of the proposed legislation, PHI isn't covered because a breach of it would not result in financial damage.

Okay, let's play along for the time being. Never mind the fact that we're only discussing a narrowly defined law because legisla-tors are terrified to propose anything that might result in costly compliance for their corporate supporters; never mind that there is nothing about encryption. The idea that any of the above areas not covered by the proposed bill won't cause financial harm can be easily brushed aside with one mind-blowing word of refutation: extortion.

The fact is that scam artists have countless tricks up their sleeves, and it's up to legislators to keep anticipating the next one. A single text or rented movie could ruin a person's life, and fraudsters know that. If the wrong person gains access to your personal data, and any of those bytes contain information that might harm you professionally or personally, they most certainly could be used against you for financial gain.

In Chapter 1, we looked at a *Science* study that showed how with just a few data points (Instagram posts and tweets), it was possible to reconnect anonymized data about credit card purchases with the unique consumer who made them. It may sound odd or offbeat to insist that a Congressional bill should cover Instagram posts, but with its narrow definition of what should be covered, the Data Security and Breach Notification Act of 2015 would offer no recourse to a person whose data has been compromised by a glitch in Instagram's code. Thus, a problem deemed by the law of the land to be "financially harmless" could empty our bank accounts overnight.

These considerations make me think what we really need in the federal government is someone in a position of authority with the expertise and knowledge to make sure anyone exposed in a breach knows about it, and is informed about the potential fallout, as far as current intel permits, as quickly as possible. Call this person a breach czar, if you will. Since data-related crimes are often quite ingenious, isn't it best to err on the side of caution?

Any federal law aimed at protecting consumers from the danger of identity-related crime needs to be best in class, far better than all the existing state laws combined, and, while it should go without saying, it also must not supersede stronger existing protections afforded by sister federal agencies.

There is still a yawning gulf between what's been done and what needs to be done in the realm of cyber legislation. The protections we deserve are a work in progress, one that the entire constellation of consumer advocates and data-security experts must solve in concert. Data-related crimes are constantly evolving, and we need to get in the habit of responding to the very biggest picture we can imagine.

Arguing about what consumers need to know regarding the way their PII is being used and stored is tedious. The fact that it's still legal for personal information to be in the possession of a third party and not be stored in an encrypted format is beyond comprehension.

Addressing this problem begins with consumer behavior. We need to weave it into the way we conduct our affairs. For consumers, that means being more circumspect about the information we put out into the world—and the way we design our response to the now everyday reality of data breaches and private details getting spilled into the publicly accessible virtual world.

"If we're going to be connected, then we need to be protected," President Obama proclaimed at the Federal Trade Commission, speaking about the Consumer Privacy Bill of Rights Act and the Student Digital Privacy Act during the lead-up to his 2015 State of the Union address. In wide-ranging remarks, the president expressed what should be a self-evident truth, but is not yet a reality in the new digital age: "As Americans, we shouldn't have to forfeit our basic privacy when we go online to do our business."

Once again, there was a lot of talk about policy, but very little in the way of a map that contained specific points on the journey to better data security. As a matter of fact, as we look to the government to get us on the right path, we can't avoid the fact that the government's woeful data practices are lost in the same no-man's land that any new legislation must address.

A recent report on data-security practices, programs, and defenses at the Department of Homeland Security points toward what may well be a horrible train wreck to come. According to the report, "Widespread weaknesses in the federal government's information security practices represent a significant vulnerability that could be exploited by adversaries, creating a potential threat to national security and American citizens."

Listed among the DHS fails are many incidents, including one from 2013, when hackers got into the U.S. Army Corps of Engineers network and downloaded "information about 85,000 dams . . . and the potential fatalities that could be caused by a breach." In another example, "The Nuclear Regulatory Commission (NRC) stored sensitive cybersecurity details for nuclear plants on an unprotected shared drive, making them more vulnerable to theft." And perhaps even more alarming, "In February 2013, hackers . . . breached the Federal Communications Commission's Emergency Broadcast System to broadcast warnings in Michigan, Montana, and North Dakota about a zombie attack." The successful attack on Centcom's Twitter account and breaches at the White House, the Department of State, and the U.S. Postal Service further make the point that the government and quasi-governmental agencies are not crushing it when it comes to cybersecurity.

One of the president's key initiatives has been the Consumer Privacy Bill of Rights Act. It's technically the second one, the first having been originally unveiled at a White House ceremony that I attended in 2012. I liked the song President Obama was singing then, and the second verse is pretty much same as the first. President Obama wants to codify privacy protections in a law that features seven guiding principles designed to empower consumers by giving them some agency regarding the way companies collect, confirm, protect, and disseminate their personal data. So far, so good. Privacy and data security aren't split up.

But while the president is to be commended for trying to prioritize the issues of identity theft protection, consumer privacy, and cybersecurity, it's hard not to notice the elephant in the room. Most federal agencies don't currently meet the guidelines Obama is hoping to establish, and there doesn't seem to be a plan of action to make the change we need, the change we want to see, or even, for that matter, a change for the better.

The most concrete and valuable proposal in the Personal Data Notification and Protection Act is the call for—you guessed it—a federal breach notification law. While many lawmakers have tried to make this happen, none have come close enough to what is actually needed. State legislatures have filled the void by enacting an inconsistent patchwork of both strong and weak breach notification laws that have different requirements and create uncertainty and confusion in the business and nonprofit communities. If Obama's plan becomes the law of the land, consumers would be guaranteed notification if their personally identifiable information was involved in a breach within thirty days of it happening, although exceptions can be made. While it would appear to preempt tougher state notification laws, the proposed legislation does permit state authorities to enforce consumer privacy protection laws that the federal bill does not cover.

"Each of us as individuals have a sphere of privacy around us that should not be breached," the president said in his remarks to the FTC, "whether by our government, but also by commercial interests."

The problem once again was that there was no "there" there in Obama's sketch of our nation's "plan" for a safer and more secure future. Indeed, the federal government doesn't even meet the requirements outlined in his proposal. And there's the rub. Obama is calling for "a single, strong national standard so Americans know when their information has been stolen or misused," but federal agencies were not specifically mentioned, and, in my opinion, one has to at least wonder if the federal government will try to take a pass.

According to a Government Accountability Office report last year, fewer than 30 percent of federal agencies comply with the proposed Personal Data Notification and Protection Act. While the U.S. Postal Service, Energy Department, State Department, and several other agencies of note have suffered significant breaches of highly sensitive personal information over the past few years, not one of them informed the individuals affected within the stipulated one-month period now advocated by the White House.

By now, almost every American has been a victim of online crime at some point—whether or not they know it. In the first quarter of 2015, there were more than 100 million records compromised.

More than a billion records containing personally identifiable information have been exposed since 2005. Yet even as consumers get hit again and again, there's been no meaningful federal action on data security.

When it comes to data breach notifications, how long is too long to wait? In the case of the infamous Target breach, company officials didn't acknowledge the compromise until a full week after they learned of it, and then only after a journalist forced their hand. Such delays are all too common, and there's no question that disclosure must be faster.

The underlying problem is a lack of federal oversight when it comes to consumer-related cybersecurity. Credit and debit card breaches are less damaging than those involving personally identifiable information. Your name, Social Security number, passwords, date of birth, medical records, home address, bank account numbers, email address, and even your transaction histories can all be found on the data black market if your information has been exposed in a breach. Any law that addresses consumer cybersecurity would have to be applicable in circumstances ranging from simple credit card breaches to a security failure at the Internal Revenue Service.

Congress has tried to address these issues, introducing bills that run the gamut from easy to tough on those businesses that store such information. And almost every state in the United States has breach notification laws on the books. It's still not enough. Since data breaches have become both plentiful and inevitable, consumers can't possibly remember which companies got hit when and how badly.

This is where government, business, and consumer interests truly intersect, pointing to the need for a law that protects all injured parties.

There are two clear problems, and a solution to both—one that could benefit businesses, consumers, and the government—may lie in legislation that has been around since 1988. It is called the Schumer box.

This legislation placed the small print of credit card agreements under a magnifying glass, highlighting the terms with the largest impact on consumers—information such as long-term rates, the annual percentage rate for purchases, and the cost of financing—and making them easier to understand. The Schumer box was to credit cards what the nutritional label was to food. It should serve as a model for data breach legislation that can create a powerful tool as we make our way through the somewhat less than halcyon days of big data.

A data breach disclosure box would provide a spur to companies and government agencies that have been lackadaisical about data security in an environment that requires white-knuckled vigilance. It would also encourage organizations to improve their breach preparedness plans so they can notify consumers sooner and provide a more transparent and empathetic response.

It would apply to all businesses and government organizations that have experienced a breach, and it could be displayed in brick-and-mortar environments, on products, or online. It would look something like a nutritional label.

The type of information provided in the data breach disclosure box should be a matter for public debate. But there are a few common-sense elements to consider:

- Has this organization been breached within the past five years?
- If yes, how many times?
- What kind of information was exposed?

- What did the organization do to help affected consumers?
- Does this organization encrypt all consumer and employee data using the most up-to-date methods?
- Does the organization have a breach notification policy?
- What types of information are consumers and citizens obligated, or not obligated, to provide?

Some will argue that the data breach disclosure box will hurt businesses. But it doesn't have to be a scarlet letter. If a company can demonstrate that it is doing everything it can to help consumers, strengthen its defenses, and maintain data according to cutting-edge standards, it becomes very attractive these days.

What Washington needs to grasp is that this issue is not a matter of red states versus blue states. When it comes to the security of our data, we are all in the same state of emergency.

PART 4
Resources and Terms

APPENDIX 1
Fraud Stories

Guilty but Not Responsible

"Every day of my life for seven years, I'm on the phone with my fraud specialist trying to figure this thing out."

Those are the words of Andrea Parker. Or I should say, those are the words of an identity theft victim whose name was changed to Andrea Parker in the media, because she was dragged through such an unmitigated hell she was scared the woman who scammed her—or worse, a new and even crueler fraudster—would decide that she makes an irresistible target.

Andrea is noteworthy because really every imaginable kind of identity theft happened to her. She was the victim of criminal identity theft—crimes were committed by someone using her name—and financial theft. On the monetary side of things, the damage was more than $40,000 in medical bills alone, but in terms of the way it impacted her life, the damage is simply unfathomable.

"It's been hell," she told a reporter in 2011, when she was working her way out of the morass created for her by a criminal.

The thief got a driver's license and a passport in Parker's name (her actual name), and committed felonies that entered the jurisprudence system using her name, so that every time she applied for a job, she failed her background check. A store got in touch with her about some shoplifting, and a bank called about some accounts that she neither set up nor knew anything about.

"Basically, she's been doing everything and anything she can do with my name. She's living as me," she told Herb Weisbaum when he covered her story in his ConsumerMan column at NBC News.

Parker had never been arrested, but there were warrants out for her arrest in California for crimes she didn't commit, and no way to go and defend herself without getting arrested in the process, since as far as law enforcement was concerned, there was only one of her, and she was a criminal.

"I never had a parking ticket," she told Keith Yaskin, a reporter with the local Fox affiliate in Phoenix, Arizona.

Meanwhile, a twenty-nine-year-old woman named Debbie Miller was arrested in Florida and accused of misusing more than $34,000 worth of Social Security benefits. Miller was Andrea Parker's identity thief.

This was a clean sweep. Every time she left her home, Parker had to worry about something as banal as a traffic stop, because it opened the possibility that her driver's license would be run through a law enforcement database, her "record" would be discovered, and a call for backup to arrest her made. My company IDT911 helped her obtain special credentials so that if she was pulled over, police on the scene would have sufficient information to prevent an arrest.

Sarah Carr, Almost IRS Scam Victim

A voice mail was waiting for Sarah Carr one not-so-fine Tuesday morning. She was very pregnant—at the tail end of her third trimester.

Expecting any day, the hormonal perfect storm raging inside her, the last thing she needed was that threatening message informing her not only that the IRS had placed a lien on her property, but that the federal government was filing tax fraud charges against her.

To say she was beside herself would be an understatement—a mom-to-be going to jail.

There was no reason to doubt the threats were real. She reasoned that there must have been an error in her tax forms, but the IRS must have decided it was an intentional act of deceit. When she called the number that the IRS agent left, she was confronted in a way that had to be real, since the agent had the type of sensitive personal information that couldn't possibly have been gleaned from the Internet—or so she thought.

Or did she think anything?

For most of us, when we get such a call, the last thing on our minds is that we are being scammed. The most common reaction is to panic, and point the finger at yourself. Scam artists bank on that. You're much more likely to think "What did I do wrong?" than "Is someone out to get me?"

But that latter response needs to become your default setting.

Sarah Carr was lucky.

She panicked while the man on the line regaled her with seemingly hard-to-know facts about her life, including serious details about the three companies that she owned. In reality, he was providing a real-life illustration of why your name, phone number, email address, and even

---

If you get a call from any institution about a financial matter or an issue regarding your information security, ask for a phone number and hang up.

Confirm that the number is correct. Many scams will turn up if you simply enter the phone number in the search box of your Internet browser. But the simplest solution is to look up the number on the organization's website—whether it is for the IRS or any other organization.

Pro tip: The IRS will never call you or send you an email. Their initial communication is always by way of snail mail.

your various identities on social media (in this case, probably her LinkedIn resume) need to be understood rightly as so many elements of your discoverable personally identifiable information. The scammer Carr was talking to was using that sort of information to scare her into sending him money.

"You hear about scams all the time, and you think that you're smart enough and you would recognize [it]," Carr told KUSA in an interview. "It was all just so real."

Then, as Carr's would-be scammer explained what was going to happen next, she started crying. It's not a tactic that will do you much good ordinarily, but Carr got lucky.

"I blurted out, 'I'm nine months pregnant. I'm supposed to have a baby in three weeks. I don't know what I'm going to do,'" Carr told KUSA, "And then he says, 'Wait, wait, wait, wait, you're pregnant?' And I said, 'Yes!' And he goes 'I'm sorry. I'm sorry. I'm sorry, this is a scam. You're OK. We're scamming you. We were just trying to get money out of you. Please stop crying.'"

And so Sarah Carr slipped the noose.

Tragically, the IRS scam is becoming more and more common, but like a good punch line, it's all in the delivery. If the right swindler gets your number, you're going to need some serious muscle memory (hang up, check the number, call back) to avoid getting got.

Nudegate

Remember when the Internet was nearly trampled to death in a digital stampede for nude celebrity photos, including pictures of Jennifer Lawrence, Ariana Grande, Mary Elizabeth Winstead, Kate Upton, Rihanna, and others? More than one hundred celebrities made that particular list of Hollywood Who's Who.

The pictures found their way online—as in the public part of the Internet—because there was demand, and a cool problem set for a hacker to solve. Most likely, the hackers exploited one of the key elements of celebrity: that everyone knows everything about their favorite stars. With a little online searching, you can find loads of seemingly innocuous information about your favorite pop star, like a sister's first name or the name of their elementary school. Identity thieves are all too happy to have it. The hackers who got ahold of the nude photos didn't need fans to grab the adored one's Social Security number. They just needed to know the name of their childhood friend, their first dog's name, the first street they lived on, or their mother's maiden name. From there, armed only with an email address, the hackers were able to penetrate each affected star's Apple iCloud account by answering security questions. Sad but true. The pictures were reportedly floating around on the deep web for a week before they hit the broader information highway.

While the FBI began investigating how the pictures found their way to the public, millions of people were feverishly searching for ways to view the purloined photos. It became harder to find the most sought-after photographs—Jennifer Lawrence topped that list—when Perez Hilton's eponymous site took them down and issued an apology—though not before a bunch of dough was made on page views.

You can probably spot a phishing email in your sleep, and you would no sooner respond to an email about suspicious activity on your credit card than you would leave your wallet in a crosswalk in Times Square.

However, best practices often fly out the window when it comes to salacious material about our favorite celebrities. Think about it this way: As you wander in the darker alleys and backstreets of the Internet, where the risks should outweigh all other considerations, are you willing to forego sensible web behavior, when the likely outcome will be catastrophic?

The first threat is malware. You can expect it to wind up on your computer if you decide to search the less safe parts of the Internet for material that was never meant for your eyes anyway.

It may be something simple, like code that turns your computer into a spam distribution center, or a more serious app that will record your keystrokes (including when you log in to your bank account). There's no way to know what you're getting yourself into. The best course of action is to use your imagination—or possibly even your sense of what should be off-limits. Malware can often lead to identity theft.

If you tend to chase breaking news stories and like to download the ephemera related to them (eyewitness photographs, blog posts), you may want to do a malware scan of your computer. As a matter of fact, this kind of scanning should be a part of your habit of monitoring your various points of contact with the outside world—your attackable surface—regularly for signs of fraud. And of course, the very least you can do is make sure that your devices are protected with highly reviewed antivirus and antimalware software that is kept up to date.

Katie Smith, Credit Card Fraud Victim

According to a report released by the U.S. Justice Department in December 2013, 45 percent of identity theft victims found out when they were contacted by a financial institution. That's how Katie Smith learned that her identity was stolen.

"They went to an outlet mall," Smith recalled, "and you could look on a map and see that they went from store to store to store to store." The miscreant who hijacked Smith's identity had it down to a science; he or she spread $18,000 worth of fraudulent charges across fourteen stores at an outlet mall.

"You feel very vulnerable. You feel out of control and someone else has stolen something from you. And it's not like they stole your car. They stole who you are. They're out there misrepresenting you, and there's definitely an emotional component to it that I didn't realize until weeks into it."

Smith had access to a dedicated fraud resolution expert who ushered her from panic to peace of mind. After about six months, all of the credit and reputational issues caused by the $18,000 shopping spree were resolved. The process would have taken far longer had she tried to resolve each of the fourteen fraudulent accounts on her own, since it requires a significant amount of time and effort to report the crime to law enforcement, communicate with the fraud departments of the credit reporting agencies, develop the requisite documentation, and then sort everything out with the various retailers where she got got.

Kathryn Birmingham, Two Cases of Identity Theft

In 2001, Kathryn Birmingham learned that someone had been using the address of a property that she and her husband owned. They weren't living there at the time. There wasn't even a house.

Whoever did it used the address to set up a number of credit accounts in the United States. Changing a physical address is the most common way fraudsters take over an account.

Kathryn discovered the situation when a number of bills were delivered to her actual residence because there was no deliverable address on the vacant property. She then began the arduous process of investigating what had happened.

"Over the next year," Birmingham said, "many bills and different connections for this one individual were established for this one property. So, I started trying to unwind it and try to do that on my own and I found that the institutions would not speak to me because I didn't have that individual's Social Security number. He had mine."

Birmingham hired a lawyer, and spent the better part of three years trying to sort out the situation, clear the property, and repossess her own address.

"It was very frustrating," she said.

Then it happened again.

"I found out that our IRS account had been hacked and I found out that it had occurred several years before and the government was just informing us of what had occurred."

The first time around, she had to sue corporations to get them to stop allowing a criminal to use her address. The second time around was easier, because she had access to a fraud resolution service through her insurance company. It's also worth noting that some time had passed—as the various crimes associated with identity theft increase, so has the ability to fight those crimes.

The most important take-away is that it's necessary to follow the Three Ms if you want to catch fraudulent activity associated with your name, Social Security number, or other personally identifiable information.

Ebony Walton, Married to a Stranger for Eighteen Years

"I now pronounce you husband and lies."

That was the first line of the *New York Post* article about Ebony Walton's shocking discovery. The thirty-five-year-old New Yorker had applied for a marriage license, having decided it was time to finally tie the knot with her high-school sweetheart and boyfriend of eighteen years. But it wasn't to be—or at least, not right away.

There was some shocking news. A clerk told Walton that she was already married, according to public records. In fact the nuptials in question had occurred eighteen years earlier, on December 10, 1997. It was an impossibility, but when she tried to tell that to the powers that be, she got nowhere.

At the time of the surprise wedding that she knew nothing about, Walton was eighteen years old and living with her boyfriend, her mother, and two cousins in a Harlem apartment. She had never heard of the person authorities said she had married, a man who hailed from Gujranwala, Pakistan. But as she came to terms with the fact that something happened, she started piecing together how it could have come to be.

A big chunk of identity-related scams are crimes of opportunity. The people who have the best shot at acquiring the kinds of information needed to pull off a caper like the one perpetrated against Ebony Walton are often those closest to us, like family and friends. That was the case here.

It was a decidedly low-tech scam. One of Walton's cousins looked enough like Walton to use her identification. There was nothing more to the matter. The unwitting wife of eighteen years readily admitted that she left her identification unprotected in the home she shared with her cousins. The cousin in question had a drug problem, and had stolen Walton's identification to register for a marriage license in a green-card marriage scam. She got the money, and Walton got the problem.

In this instance, it wasn't too difficult to unravel. Judge John Spooner of the Office of Administrative Trials and Hearings in New York found that Ebony had been a victim of identity theft and green-lighted her marriage.

Yehuda Katz, NYPD Auxiliary Cop Scam Artist Supreme

This is not a common scam, but it's a cautionary tale that illustrates what should be an axiom by now: We are beyond the point of "trust but verify" when it comes to unsolicited phone calls.

Today the credo should go something like, "Assume the worst, and remain suspicious even when you're relatively sure—having hung up, poked around the Internet, called the main number of whatever organization allegedly called you, and asked yourself, 'Does this make sense?'"

Yehuda Katz drove to and from work in a black Cadillac with the custom license plates, KATZILAC. He was an NYPD auxiliary deputy inspector based in Brooklyn and the epitome of what you might imagine an ambulance chaser to be—but he wasn't a lawyer. He was nothing short of a parasite.

That said, he was a clever parasite.

Yehuda Katz hacked into the NYPD computer and law enforcement databases to get information associated with people who had been involved in traffic accidents. He grabbed their information from police reports and contacted them, claiming to be a lawyer.

Katz's calls and letters included statements like, "I can advise you with 100% confidence that I can resolve this claim in your favor." While it is unclear how he made money, the disgraced cop logged a lot of calls to medical clinics, law firms, and chiropractors that pointed toward some kind of kickback racket.

All told, the Katzilac-driving lout made more than 6,400 searches between May and August 2014 by hacking into computers at the seventieth precinct in Brooklyn, where he had installed a camera so he would know when he could enter the system without being detected. The discovery of that camera was his undoing.

What about the people he duped? They learned the *Bad Lieutenant* version of the NYPD public messaging, "Courtesy, Professionalism, Respect," where all it takes is one cop to protect his car payments by self-serving in a poorly protected law enforcement information trough.

Catphishing

While we're running the gamut here, there really are two main categories of vulnerability when it comes to identity theft: finance (which should be self-explanatory) and romance.

Nowhere is the romance category more an issue than online.

Studies have shown that more than 80 percent of all people lie (not to mention use Photoshop-primped pictures) in their online dating profiles. For those of you who haven't yet dipped your toe into the tepid water of online dating, trust me. Most dating site users can tell a tale of woe regarding a less-than-forthcoming digital love interest who, when a face-to-face encounter occurred, wasn't everything he or she seemed.

A little white lie here or there during the courting phase is standard operating procedure for many, but it's also a common tactic for people who are looking for something other than love. Scammers who lie about who they are—and their romantic intentions—solely to get access to someone's PII are a growing problem, and they certainly can be added to the roster of other notable phishing scams.

One of the more famous catphishing victims is Notre Dame football star Manti Te'o, whose heart-wrenching story of a love gained and lost was splashed across television screens from one end of the country to the other. Straight out of a Disney script, they met in Palo Alto after a game and fell in love. There was a car accident, a diagnosis of leukemia, love letters written, countless unending phone conversations, and then a tragic death.

According to Timothy Burke and Jack Dickey of Deadspin, the object of Te'o's affection was a catphisher. There is no record of her birth, no record of her being a student at Stanford, no record of her car accident, no record of her death, no obituary, and the only photographs that identify her are snapshots from a social media account of a twenty-two-year-old living in California who is still alive and has a different name than the woman Te'o professed to be in love with.

Former Denver Nuggets star Chris Anderson faced a criminal investigation after a woman pretended to be him online and scammed and blackmailed more than a dozen victims (including a woman with whom he had a real-life relationship). A mother-daughter team in Colorado squeezed more than $1 million out of more than three hundred women around the world by pretending to be American soldiers who needed a few bucks to buy a phone or a plane ticket.

As the Better Business Bureau has warned, these scams are on the rise, in part because they're cheap and easy. Many online dating sites are free to users, fake photos are easy to find, and a little investment—whether in time spent or in flower deliveries, neither of which requiring that a person be present—can net more in financial returns from the charmed women or men who fall under a catphisher's spell.

So how do you make yourself somewhat invulnerable to catphishing? Psychologist Jack Schafer warns people to be wary of truth bias, our innate belief that most people are telling the truth in the absence of evidence to the contrary.

But there are some more concrete tips you can follow if you want to be safe from catphishers.

- Be wary of romantic interest from someone who says they can't meet. He's really American but lives abroad right now (but is using OKCupid and contacting people in your city). Her phone got shut off. His webcam won't work. Scammers always have a hundred arrows in their cupid's quiver of reasons why you can't meet them in person, talk on the phone, or even see them on a webcam, and they're almost all disguising the fact that they're using another person's picture and a made-up identity to woo you. Before you let yourself get too sucked into a whirlwind romance with a would-be Romeo or Juliet, make sure the person you think you're falling for is more than just a few ghostwritten love letters and a model's picture.
- Be suspicious of someone who always has emergencies. Once a catphisher thinks she or he has hooked a live one, they'll test their mark to see how far they can push the trust they've worked hard to build. (It doesn't hurt that this can play into their efforts to avoid actually having to meet, talk, or be seen.) But while having emergencies is a

fact of life, involving people who don't really know you in them really isn't—and asking for money to resolve them is really bad form.

- Never turn over personal information or pictures you wouldn't want widely available. Maybe your new squeeze-muffin will suddenly ask for a credit card number to buy a plane ticket, inquire about where your bank is located, or request something like your Social Security or passport number. Maybe they'll ask you for pictures of you in compromising situations, or to engage in some racy video chats. While giving out your personal information is enough of an identity gamble, don't ignore the increased risk of having your personal pictures or screengrabs used against you as blackmail by a catphisher out for more than just titillation.

- Don't give someone money, or help him or her access money. Alarm bells should start going off the moment any potential romantic partner asks you for even a smidge of financial assistance. His or her first request might be small—perhaps something to help take care of an emergency situation—but most catphishers quickly accelerate their requests for money. If you refuse to help, they might ask you to deposit a check or accept a wire transfer from a friend and pass the money along, but the money you're supposed to get never really arrives or the check bounces, leaving you holding the bag.

- Never click strange links or download files you receive. Even the most heartfelt-seeming e-card can mask something more dangerous than an online-only romance: weird links to unfamiliar sites or files you're asked to download can contain malware or viruses that do more than just spam your computer with ads. You could end up with a keystroke logger on your system, which would allow the sender to see passwords to everything (including your checking account), or a virus that turns your computer into a botnet to launch attacks against other sites. If you don't really know the person, don't trust the file (and, sometimes, even if you do know the person, don't trust the file).

We have all been in situations where romantic flights of fantasy can lead us on journeys that may not have fairytale endings. When the tiny alarm bell starts going off in your head, listen carefully, lest your love boat turns into the *Titanic*.

Military Scams

There is a special circle of hell reserved for those who would perpetrate identity theft on active duty personnel.

For years the military has used Social Security numbers for everything from identifying duffel bags to checking out a rifle at the shooting range. Based on a directive issued a few years back, our armed forces are beginning to kick their SSN addiction. However, there are lingering effects, and the crime of identity theft can represent a huge problem for our service men and women.

The Three Ms are very important for our service men and women. There is just too much of their information flowing through too many hands. Many members of the military, as well as civilian contractors who work for the military or the U.S. government, must access classified information, and to do that they must obtain specific levels of security clearances—and they are not easy to pass. To join the ranks of this relatively elite group of people with serious access, an employee has to authorize the government to do the equivalent of a PII/PHI strip search (as well it should be), including the right to vet a candidate and to examine their employment history, medical history, and any criminal records and personal finances. All that information is potentially get-table, and if it gets got, the person with whom it is associated is in big trouble.

If a member of the military becomes a victim of identity theft, his or her world can be thrown into disarray. A single case of criminal identity theft—such as that experienced by Andrea Parker—can mean that security clearances are denied or revoked. According to my colleague Eva Velasquez, president and CEO of the Identity Theft Resource Center, if an enlisted person is in the process of applying for a new position, he or she will be disqualified from consideration. A bad credit score can do the trick. This is why it's so crucial to observe the Three Ms.

When a person's identity portfolio has been compromised, a background check can reveal a resume that has been turned into a rap sheet—arrests, tax crimes, and credit scores hammered by late payments and maxed-out payment cards. The entirety of who you are (on paper at least) can be laid waste by identity thieves moving about the country, doing whatever they damn please while leaving a trail of PII crumbs that lead back to an innocent victim.

Velasquez wrote a fascinating article about the case of an Air National Guardsman in Alabama. Major Zane Purdy made six figures a year working for a defense contractor until his identity was stolen and sold to a tax fraud ring. The result was the loss of his job and suspension from the National Guard. Obviously, his security clearance was also revoked. His next job, working at a restaurant, paid $7.25 an hour.

The issues that face enlisted men and women when it comes to identity theft and identity-related crimes are many. In response to the threats out there, the Department of Veterans Affairs created an identity theft education program to bring military personnel up to speed on what they need to know to stay safe.

The military is no stranger to breaches. Over the years there have been a number of incidents reported at bases around the country. Thieves have accessed databases of active duty personnel deployed in Europe, Iraq, and Afghanistan. There have been compromises of government contractors that do background checking for various military and government agencies.

The Identity Theft Resource Center recommends that military personnel take the following actions to protect their identities and their security clearances:

- **Put an active-duty alert on your credit reports.** Similar to a fraud alert, it requires a prospective borrower to provide additional verification to open a new line of credit. The ITRC has a template letter to help service men and women who wish to take advantage of this protection.

- **Grant a power of attorney to a spouse or loved one before you depart.** Be sure to choose a trustworthy and responsible individual who has your best interests in mind. Keep in mind that a large percentage of identity theft occurs among friends and family, so choose wisely.

- **Think about working with an identity management service.** Contact your insurance agent, bank or credit union representative, the HR Department at work, or the appropriate department for your service branch to see if they provide access to such a program. Do your research and make sure that it offers the features you need, such as credit monitoring for you and your immediate family and resolution services in the event you need them.

If you are in the military, there is only so much your employer can do to help you after your identity has been stolen and used. That's why you need to be proactive in your defense, have a monitoring process in place, and know how to contain the damage if the worst happens.

Identity Theft's Senior Moment

According to the AARP, statistics show that senior citizens are tasty targets for identity thieves. Perhaps more so than other age groups.

According to my colleague Brett Montgomery at IDT911, the *Florida Times-Union* reported that one reason seniors are so attractive to identity thieves is that many find checkbooks preferable to debit or credit cards, and, of course, online purchases are completely anathema to them.

So what's this about back checks? The humble back check (your check cashed and canceled and returned with your monthly statement) is a cornucopia of personally identifiable information: name, address, bank address, account number, and routing number. This may not exactly be the Holy Grail for criminals who are looking to set themselves up to do fraudulent electronic wire transfers, but it's pretty good.

The *Times-Union* article went on to warn that receiving a check can be a problem—one that many seniors may overlook. What can look like a refund or reward is actually a contract of sorts. Read the small print on the check, because it might tell you precisely what sort of misdeed is about to be done by cashing it. It could be the recipient is confirming their enrollment in some type of plan that automatically deducts money from their account each month, for just one example. Checks are not a one-way street when it comes to personally identifiable information.

Look at the back of a deposited check—one of your own—and you will see both the account number and routing number of the recipient—another clever way to gather personal information from an elderly mark.

Oftentimes scammers will contact seniors by phone. They will pose as someone calling from the government, a charity, a retailer, or law enforcement—all that can vary wildly—but one thing all these callers will have in common is that they will either ask for money or the types of personal information that put a senior in harm's way—or, more often, they will ask for both. Simple advice: No senior—or anyone else, for that matter—should provide any information to anyone who calls looking for it. They should only authenticate themselves if they make the call and are in control of the conversation.

Another soft spot in a senior's attackable surface is the frailty of old age itself. There have been a variety of scams perpetrated on seniors by their home healthcare providers. As an elderly person peacefully dozes off in their favorite chair, the fraudster can go rifling through files, combing through drawers, looking through the mail, and grabbing sensitive documents, checkbooks, or Social Security checks.

Not only should seniors or their families ask home healthcare agencies to confirm that they have thoroughly checked the backgrounds of anyone they send to their homes, children should consider convincing their elderly relatives to activate credit freezes whenever they put themselves under the constant care of another. That is particularly important when a senior goes into an assisted living facility.

APPENDIX 2

A Glossary of Scams

Account Takeover

This is a popular one (for fraudsters) and a serious source of woe. Using login credentials—often procured from a data breach—the scammer gets control of an account and maxes it out.

Caller ID Scam

You receive a phone call from a person, company, utility, or other organization, but how do you know who's really calling? It's on your caller ID, of course. But since caller IDs are easily customized, you have absolutely no way of knowing who's actually calling you. You might even receive a phone call from yourself, based on the number on the screen! Scammers can easily manipulate the information on the phone to appear to be anyone they choose, and unfortunately, it's our trust in technology that makes us vulnerable to scams.

If anyone ever calls you and requests money, hang up. No legitimate business transaction will take place when the company calls *you* and requests payment. If there's a chance that there's some validity to it, end the call and contact the company yourself, using an established phone number that you independently confirm.

If a caller ever tells you that you can trust him because the number came up on your caller ID, hang up immediately. A genuine representative of a company would be able to provide you with not only a phone number to call, but an employee number or some other form of verification. (ITRC)

Car Ad Wrap Scam

You get an email offering a fantastic opportunity from Monster energy drinks, Heineken, or Coca-Cola. You can earn $1,500 just by driving your car after it's wrapped with an advertisement for their brand. You receive a check for an amount far exceeding your agreed-upon compensation, and when you ask about it, you're told that the extra money is for the design of the ad wrap. You're provided with instructions for wiring the money to the designer. Here's the problem: It was a bad check, and now you're on the hook with your bank for the amount you forwarded to the designer.

Car History Scam

You've probably seen commercials for helpful services like CARFAX that show potential buyers the damage and service histories on previously owned vehicles. Unfortunately, there's a new scam out there that involves getting you to buy this kind of service history.

This scam mostly occurs when you try to sell a vehicle online, although it could happen in person or in response to a classified ad. You're contacted by someone who seems genuinely interested in your car. He says all the right things, doesn't come across as pushy or shady, and wants specific info on your vehicle. One of his requests is that you provide a car history, and he's even kind enough to send you a link to one of the cheapest and most comprehensive history report sites out there.

The problem is, he makes a commission for getting you to purchase this history. Once you've bought it from that site, provided one from a different site, or refused, he changes his mind and no longer wants to buy the car. He's made his money, so he doesn't need you anymore.

Tip: It's a good idea to have the vehicle history before placing an ad for your car. It demonstrates that you're a genuine seller who is being transparent about the vehicle's quality and value, and it will protect you from this type of scam. If you're not including that fee in the sale of your vehicle, just remember that this scam is out there and that affiliates work the Internet to make their commissions. (ITRC)

Check Fraud

This old-fashioned swindle has new life: ATMs often provide a receipt that includes the image of the check you've deposited. Throw that in the trash, and an identity thief has the name, address, and bank account information of the person or entity that issued the check.

Child Identity Theft

Children have Social Security numbers, which makes them prime targets for identity theft. Often the scams go undetected for more than a decade because kids don't check their credit reports and most parents assume it's unnecessary.

The problem is that anyone who is close to that child can hijack his or her information. It happens more to children in foster care, but anyone—including family and friends—with sufficient access can grab that information and run wild with it. In the past year, due to the megabreaches of Anthem and Premera, the PII of hundreds of thousands, if not millions, of children has been stolen by hackers, putting them in harm's way.

Counterfeit Cards and Card-Not-Present Transactions

You're driving and your phone rings. You answer it with hands-free, catching only a glimpse of the caller ID—or none at all. The caller sounds like so many other customer service representatives. She asks, "Mr. _____. This is _____ bank. Is this your credit card number? Is this your expiration date? Your account has been marked by security for possible fraud. We need to confirm the card is in your possession. Can you confirm your security code, please?"

Credit Card Fraud

This is of course the most common form of identity theft, and there are many variations. Maybe you handed your credit card to a waiter to settle your bill, gave it to a bartender to start a tab, dropped it in the back seat of a cab, or recited the digits to someone over the phone when ordering food for delivery.

While you're having a good time at the bar or relaxing at home, your order wending its way to you, that card number has been captured, written down along with the expiration date and security code.

Credit Card Insurance Scam

You receive a call from a "company" that offers credit card insurance. You think it's weird since credit cards are already insured by the issuer and the person who calls you wants a sizeable fee. Hang up. If you don't, what comes next is a request for your personally identifiable information.

Tip: Never give your banking information or Social Security number to anyone over the telephone unless you have initiated the call to a known company or organization. Also, as most credit card companies offer insurance programs for their cardholders, purchasing additional insurance from another "company" is frivolous and often leads to identity theft. (ITRC)

Debit Card Fraud

You try to pay with your debit card and the cashier tells you that the charge was declined due to insufficient funds—but you know there was money in your account. There are a thousand ways to max out a card, but most credit card companies offer zero-liability protection these days. Not so with all debit cards, where you can be on the hook for $500 or the entire amount stolen, depending on how long the fraud went unreported.

Debt Tagging

This is a debt collection scam that can cause you endless headaches. A junk debt buyer purchases bad debt and looks for anyone with the same name as the name on the debt—the more common your name, the more likely the sting—and then they use aggressive tactics, including the threat of filing a collection action on your credit report, if you don't pay.

Disaster Scams

A natural disaster brings out the very best and the very worst in people.

Posing as charity workers, fraudsters troll neighborhoods looking for unguarded houses to rob. A home improvement contractor may knock on your door offering to do repair work at bargain-basement prices, with the goal of getting a large deposit and skipping town.

"Neighbors" you have never seen before show up offering to help you clean up the inside of your home, then steal your sensitive personal documents.

You may be forced out of your home and take refuge in the home of a friend, neighbor, family member, or just a good Samaritan. If you do, keep your personal documents close to you and as secure as possible, lest they fall into the hands of an identity thief looking to take advantage of your distraction and vulnerability at a time of crisis.

Donation Overpayment Scheme

According to the Internet Crime Complaint Center (IC3), many businesses, charitable organizations, schools, universities, health-related organizations, and nonprofit organizations reported an online donation scheme. Thousands of dollars of donations were made to unwitting organizations through stolen credit cards. Once the donations were received, the fake contributors immediately requested the majority of the donation back, but credited to a different card, claiming to have mistakenly donated too much by adding an extra digit to the dollar amount (e.g., $5,000 was "accidently" entered instead of $500). Very few of the complainants actually returned the money to the second credit card. Many, through their own investigations, discovered the original card was stolen, or the credit card company notified them of such. Also, some of the organizations' policies did not allow funds to be returned to a different credit card. (ITRC/IC3)

Email Scams

Email scams come in a wide variety of formats, but each essentially works in one of a handful of ways. The goals include gaining access to your personally identifiable information by having you fill out "necessary" forms; gaining access to your money by having you send in a "shipping and handling" fee or to pay taxes before receiving a prize; or having you click on a link to see what you've won, only to have the link contain malicious software that infects your computer and steals your information.

Here are some sure signs that the email is a scam:

- **Money for Nothing:** *No one* is going to contact you out of the blue and give you loads of money. It's nice to dream about, but it's simply not the reality. They're also not going to contact you online from a free email address.
- **Dear Sir or Madam:** Think about it: If someone was genuinely going to give you millions of dollars, wouldn't they know your name?
- **Youve Alredy One!:** Typos and poor grammar are dead giveaways that something isn't right about this email. If the sender's job is to inform people all day long that they're now millionaires, wouldn't they spell it right?
- **Hurry, This Offer Is Only Good for the Next Ten Seconds:** Sorry, but if you're the verified winner of a large sum of money or, even better, the recipient of an inheritance, there's no ten-second deadline. If your long-lost great-great-aunt stipulated in her will that you had ten seconds to respond, something funny's going on.
- **Just Send Us the Processing Fee:** If you ever win anything that requires *you* to pay money, it's a scam, whether in an email or in real life. Winners don't pay before receiving their prizes; even multimillion-dollar lottery winners only pay a portion of the winnings to the IRS after claiming their prizes.
- **Funny, I Don't Even Remember Signing Up for This Contest:** That's because you didn't. Scammers got your name from any number of online sources. They send out these emails to thousands of people a day, hoping to get a bite. Don't take their bait.

Tip: While it would be wonderful to check your email on your lunch break and find out you could walk into your boss's office and quit, it's simply not real. Don't become a victim of these scammers. Laugh at the message if you want, let your mind wander to visions of escaping to your own private island if that's your idea of a dream getaway, then delete the email.

Emailed Receipt Scam

This scam employs a phishing tactic based on the fact that so many consumers use major chain stores like Walmart or online retailers like iTunes or Amazon. Scammers are counting on you being a frequent customer of these kinds of stores, and then clicking on their emailed attachment.

The attached receipt promised in the email is actually malicious software, which you just downloaded by opening it.

Tip: Never click a link in an email unless you were expecting it, even if it's from a friend (as their account could have been hacked in order to get you to click on it, thinking it's trustworthy). If you think you might actually have a receipt coming from that store, or you're afraid someone made a purchase on your account and this receipt may be the proof of that, then go directly to your account yourself, log in, and check your recent purchases. (ITRC)

Extended Warranty Scam

If you own any type of high-end product or appliance like a vehicle or refrigerator, you've probably already received this scam offer. It comes in a very official-looking mailer, usually one whose sides you have to tear off to open. Inside is a small amount of information about your vehicle or appliance, along with a threat that your warranty is about to expire. This company is generous enough to sell you a new extended warranty, but only if you ACT NOW!

If you call the toll-free number on the mailer, you'll be connected to a representative who gives you a fast-paced, high-pressure sales pitch to choose one of their warranty options. After taking all of your information and your initial deposit to initiate your warranty, they're done with you. Not only do they have your money and your personal information (which they can then use for identity theft), you don't receive any coverage on your purchased item whatsoever.

Remember, no one is going to contact you and offer you years of coverage for only a few hundred dollars. (ITRC)

E-ZPass® Phishing Scam

A victim receives an email stating they have not paid their toll bill. The email gives instructions to download the invoice by using the link provided, but the link is actually a .zip file that contains malware. (ITRC/IC3)

Facebook Notifications

Since Facebook users sign up for an account with their emails, it's not uncommon to receive legitimate emails informing you of activity on your account (you might actually get so many of these emails that you want to turn off the notifications in your Facebook settings). Unfortunately, scammers know that, and they have been sending out emails claiming to be from Facebook with subject lines such as, "All unread messages will be deleted."

If you receive an email from Facebook that states there are messages in your inbox that are about to expire, there's a simple solution: Head on over to Facebook and check your inbox for yourself.

Since it's not likely that this is a legitimate message, and since it's incredibly likely that the conveniently provided link in the scammer's email is going to install malicious software on your computer, delete the message immediately.

Fake Rebates

This one works either by phone or by email, and it's nothing more than a high-pressure sales pitch whose aim is to get you to hand over your information. Callers posing as employees (often of genuine, well-known companies) call you and offer you a limited-time rebate deal: If you act now, you'll be eligible for a massive rebate on their services. All it takes to lock in your rebate offer is the activation of your account.

Here's the catch: If you tell them you want to take a little while to think it over, the pressure begins. They can't guarantee the rate, or spots are filling up fast and you won't be put on the list if you don't act now. They'll tell you anything to get you to act right at that moment, but since the caller isn't actually an employee of the company, he's really just stealing your information.

If you're ever pressured to make a snap decision by a telemarketer or through an email offer, hang up or ignore it. Any genuine deal from a legitimate company will give you more than ten seconds to decide! (ITRC)

Farcing

This is nothing more than using social engineering to gather sensitive personal information from victims who become unwitting coconspirators in the theft of their own identities. In this simple scam, a fraudster sets up a fake account on, say, Facebook or Instagram, and starts friending people. Once in, he or she has access to all the information needed to build a dossier on you, or even enough in some instances to proceed straight into a credit fraud.

Grandparent Scam

Elderly persons receive phone calls where the callers claim their "relative" is in a legal or financial crisis.

Scammers claim that a relative has been arrested or was in a car accident in another country. Scammers often pose as the relative, create a sense of urgency, and make a desperate plea to victims for money. It is not unusual for scammers to beg victims not to tell other family members about the situation.

The scammers also impersonate third parties, such as an attorney, law enforcement officer, or U.S. embassy representative.

Once potential victims appear to believe the caller's story, they are provided instructions to wire money to an individual, often referred to as a bail bondsman, for their relative to be released.

Some people have reported that the callers claimed to be from countries including but not limited to Canada, Mexico, Haiti, Guatemala, and Peru.

Callers often disguise themselves by using telephone numbers generated by free applications or by spoofing their numbers.

If you receive this type of call, take a breath. Resist the temptation to act quickly. Before sending any money, attempt to contact your relative to determine whether the call is legitimate.

Never wire money based on a request made over the phone or in an email, especially to an overseas location. Wiring money is like giving cash—once you send it, you can't get it back.

Individuals who have fallen victim to this type of scam are encouraged to file a complaint with the Internet Crime Complaint Center at www.ic3.gov. (ITRC)

Green Energy

There is a booming business out there for legitimate companies trying to help consumers reduce their carbon footprint with cleaner energy, but there are also fraudsters who pretend to do it. Companies that resell clean energy may also go door to door. Some plans are good; some are ways to take your money up front and deliver nothing at all.

Hotel Front Desk Scam

Your plane got in late, you couldn't get a taxi, and by the time you arrived at your hotel all you wanted to do was take a shower and go to bed. About an hour after checking in, the phone in your room rings. It's the front desk calling to tell you that the credit card you gave them was declined. "Can you please read me your credit card number again? Or, if you would prefer, you can give me another credit card."

Hotel Pizza Scam

When you check into your hotel you see flyers in the lobby, or under your door, for a pizza joint. It's late and you're starving, so you call the number on the flyer. Someone answers exactly the way you expect they will. You place your order. They ask for your credit card number, which you immediately provide because your mind is on the pie and not your PII. Several hours later, you're still waiting. Starving. And unfortunately, the only one who is feeding is the thief.

Infected Pop-Up Messages

If you only share one piece of news today, make it this. It's unfathomable how many people a year fall victim to pop-up ads on their computers that "warn" them that their computers are infected. These little boxes have scary terminology and ominous designs, and it's easy to see why someone might be tempted to click, especially when the pop-ups promise to clean the computer. These can include warnings that the computer has a virus, that the Internet is running slowly, and more.

First of all, if you have solid antivirus software and an updated subscription on your computer, you won't have to worry about viruses, real or imagined. You probably also won't see these little pop-ups, since the ads themselves are a form of malicious software that you accidentally downloaded. But more importantly, clicking on the ads themselves actually *installs* malicious software like viruses. If you receive these messages or have reason to believe your computer is infected, get a recognized antivirus tool to clean it out instead of falling for this scam. (ITRC)

iPhone Code Cracker

Think your lost iPhone or iPad is safe because you locked it remotely? Think again. There is a $300 device called an IP Box that strong-arms Apple's defenses. How it works: The box tries a four-digit code, but instead of attempting passcodes manually on the touchscreen, it uses a USB to enter them. When an attempt is wrong, the box turns off the phone, which stops it from recording the failed attempt. It might take a few days—each PIN try takes forty seconds—but the phone will eventually be cracked.

IRS Scam

It's bad enough when you get a letter from the Internal Revenue Service, but getting a phone call?

The caller may tell you that you're in big trouble or that there's a small deficiency on your return, but either way they're calling because you owe money.

Scams vary. It could be the U.S. Marshal's Service has been instructed to arrest you, or a softer pedal with more nuance. They may yell, threaten, or sweet-talk you, but one thing is consistent: You need to pay, via credit card, the total amount now, before you get off the phone.

Spoiler alert: The IRS never initiates contact by phone, so you can be certain that you are in the process of getting got.

The Ishings

I call it the scourge of the "ishings": phishing, spearphishing, vishing, and smishing. Pick your poison here. Each scheme depends on luring you into clicking on the wrong link, downloading the wrong app, answering the wrong question, or providing too much information to someone you don't know (even if you think you do). Phishing does this with spam emails containing a link that downloads and installs malware or lures you to a clone website where you're asked to enter your PII. Spearphishing does it with emails that appear to come from companies with which you do business, employers, friends, and many other entities. Vishing is conducted by phone (you're actually interacting with a fraudster, automated or human), and smishing gathers your data by luring you via text message (also known as SMS). The goal is to liberate enough of your personally identifiable information to make the scammers money, or provide enough background for thieves to commit medical identity theft, criminal identity theft, child identity theft, tax refund fraud, or any number of life-changing crimes.

Jury Scam

The Jury Commissioner's Office is on the phone. It's time for you to do your civic duty. Maybe they say they need information to confirm whether you are eligible to serve on a jury. Maybe they are calling to say that you missed your report date and there's a warrant for your arrest. Whatever the question or the problem happens to be, the solution will always require the disclosure of your personally identifiable information, with your Social Security number being the main target.

Life Alert® Scam

You may have seen commercials for the Life Alert* system, the wearable button that users can press in an emergency. This system has helped countless seniors and their family members find peace of mind by knowing that help is there at the touch of a button.

Unfortunately, scammers have flipped the tables on the security that Life Alert* provides, and instead are using promises of a free Life Alert* system to steal senior citizens' identities. It works like this: The call from an automated system promises a free Life Alert*, and to receive it you simply have to press a button to speak with an operator.

Once the representative comes on the line, he or she asks for a great deal of personally identifiable information, including your address, credit card number, Medicare number (which is actually your Social Security number), and more. You never receive a free system, and the thief just made off with your identity.

Remember that legitimate businesses are moving away from automated cold calls thanks to the National Do Not Call Registry. While there are still telemarketers out there calling on behalf of companies, no telemarketer should ever ask for that level of personal information. If they do, hang up immediately. (ITRC)

LinkedIn Job Offer Scam

While social media scams on outlets like Facebook are so common they're losing their effectiveness, more serious social media sites—like the professionally oriented business community LinkedIn—are starting to be used for some pretty outrageous scams. One that has come up recently involves being messaged by one of your connections with a job offer.

First of all, the whole point of LinkedIn is to maintain connections throughout your field or industry, so these kinds of messages aren't uncommon. That's why the scam works so well. Unfortunately, the person contacting you has actually hacked into your friend's account and is sending a phony job offer. The job itself entails something illegal: to accept payments on behalf of a major-name corporation who doesn't currently have the financial right to conduct business in your region. You're to take the payments from customers and send the company the money, but withhold a percentage of the payment for yourself. Unfortunately, the people who are "ordering" these products are the scammers. They send you a check, you wire the remainder to the fake company account out of your own finances, and then the check bounces.

Tip: As with every possible scam scenario, listen to your instincts. There is no such thing as easy money, and you will never be contacted online to be given something for free. (ITRC)

Make Money from Home Scam: Students

College students have been receiving emails to their school accounts recruiting them for payroll or human resource positions with fictitious companies. The "position" simply requires the student to provide his or her bank account number to receive a deposit and then transfer a portion of the funds to another bank account.

Unbeknownst to the student, the other account is involved in the scam that the student has now helped perpetrate. The funds the student receives and then directs elsewhere have been stolen by cybercriminals. Participating in the scam is a crime and could lead to the student's bank account being closed due to fraudulent activity or federal charges.

There are actually legitimate careers that you can do from home, but you *must* do your homework and remember that no one is going to pay you to do something an automated piece of software could do for free. If it sounds too good to be true, run! (ITRC)

Make Money from Home Scam: Working Mothers

Many of the work-from-home scams are marketed specifically to working mothers because the thieves believe they are more likely to fall for it. These are online ads that include testimonials, articles supposedly published in major newspapers, and more, so who wouldn't risk $15 for a sales kit if it means keeping your little ones out of daycare and providing for your family at the same time?

Unfortunately, that $15 investment isn't even a drop in the bucket. The fine print says you owe hundreds of dollars in "membership fees" that the company just charged to your credit card. If you try to contact them to get your money back, you're going to find that the process is a full-time job by itself! (ITRC)

Malware Scams

It might be an email you get from a friend with a picture from their latest vacation; an online appeal from a charity raising money to aid victims of the latest natural disaster; a banner ad offering a free iPhone or iPad; a post on a friend's Facebook page; an emergency alert from a retailer where you have recently shopped, notifying you of a breach and directing you to a URL where you will be enrolled in a credit monitoring service; or a call from Microsoft's tech support, alerting you to an issue on your computer that can be resolved by downloading a particular program. What do these things have in common? They are designed to get you to do something that ultimately will cause you to unwittingly download malware onto your computer. If you don't catch it, it can turn your machine into a zombie botnet for spammers (sending more infected emails out to other people from your address) or a keystroke logger to capture your user ID and password as well as every stitch of your personal or financial information.

"Man in the Email" Fraud

This scheme gets its name from the "man in the middle" scam.

Companies are led to believe they are sending money to an established supply partner in China. In reality, fraudsters intercept legitimate emails between the purchasing and supply companies, and then spoof subsequent emails, impersonating each company to the other. The fraudulent emails direct the purchasing companies to send payments to a new bank account because of a purported audit. The bank accounts belong to the fraudsters, not the supply companies.

Under this scam, both companies in a legitimate business relationship can be victimized. The supplier may first ship out the legitimately ordered products and then never receive payment (because the purchasing company was scammed into paying the scammer-controlled bank account). Or the purchasing company may first make a payment and then never receive the ordered goods (because the supply company never receives that payment).

The FBI has provided some of the ways businesses can reduce their chance of being scammed by this man-in-the-email fraud:

- Establish other communication channels, such as telephone calls, to verify significant transactions. Arrange this second-factor authentication early in the relationship and outside the email environment to avoid interception by a hacker.
- Utilize digital signatures in email accounts. Be aware that this will not work with web-based email accounts, and some countries ban or limit the use of encryption.
- Avoid free, web-based email. Establish a company website domain and use it to establish company email accounts in lieu of free, web-based accounts.
- Do not use the "Reply" option to respond to unfamiliar business emails, and always double-check the address

you're sending to. Instead, use the "Forward" option and either type in the correct email address or select it from your email address book to ensure the real email address is used.

- Immediately delete unsolicited email (spam) from unknown parties. Do not open spam email, click on links in the email, or open attachments.
- Beware of sudden changes in business practices. For example, if you are suddenly asked to contact a representative at their personal email address when all previous official correspondence has been on a company email, verify via other channels that you are still communicating with your legitimate business partner.

If you or your business has been targeted by the man-in-the-email fraud, report it to the Internet Crime Complaint Center (IC3) at www.ic3.gov. The following information is helpful to report:

- Header information from email messages
- Identifiers for the perpetrator (e.g., name, website, bank account, or email addresses)
- Details on how, why, and when you believe you were defrauded
- Actual and attempted loss amounts
- Other relevant information you believe is necessary to support your complaint
- Reference to the man-in-the-email fraud (ITRC/IC3)

Medical Identity Theft

This is one of the least understood strains of identity theft, and while it is less common than credit card fraud, it's incredibly difficult to detect and resolve. Here a fraudster uses the victim's personally identifiable information in order to obtain medical treatment, acquire medical devices, get prescription medications, or gain access to their medical insurance.

The reasons behind these scams vary, and it can happen as a last-ditch effort to acquire a life-saving procedure, but often the goal is to acquire treatment that might result in an arrest or a divorce, such as a gunshot wound or a sexually transmitted disease.

The ultimate danger here is that the health information of the thief or their customer could become comingled with that of the victim, resulting in a changed—and now incorrect—blood type, or the disappearance of allergies to certain medications, which can put lives in jeopardy.

Movie Download/Rental Scam

This one has been making the rounds via iTunes, but it's surely just a matter of time before Amazon Instant Video, Redbox, and other streaming services get pulled into the scam as well.

You receive a very official-looking email from iTunes (or the other guys) with a subject line that says something like, "Your receipt #672340 for [Insert Movie Name Here]." You open the email to see what this receipt is, only to find that you were charged an outrageous amount of money to rent a movie or two. Of course, the kind folks who sent the email have a prominent link for you to click in order to challenge the transaction, since you obviously didn't make it.

The link, of course, is the real problem. It's not taking you to the customer service department, it's taking you to the scammer's own destination. There are two dangers here: The first is that you're downloading harmful viruses when you click the link, but the other is that the link may take you to what looks like a legitimate customer complaint form. Once you fill out the form, you just handed all of your personal information (and passwords, banking info, etc.) to the scammer.

If you receive an emailed receipt that you suspect isn't legitimate, ignore it and go to your account yourself. Check out your recent transactions and see if you've been charged for any unexpected rentals or purchases. Of course, you can also forward the email you received to that company's phishing department for verification. (ITRC)

Office Repair Scam

You receive a call at work that claims to be from a copy machine (or other type of office equipment) company, and the caller states there is an updated manual for your machine. All he needs is the serial number or model number from your office's system. But instead of a user manual, your office receives a box filled with expensive toner cartridges (or other accessory, depending on the machine), along with an invoice for a hefty bill. Even if your office isn't going to pay it, you're stuck trying to ship it back.

First, remember that most copiers are serviced under a contract, so only conduct business or share information with the company with which your place of business has a contract. Next, try this: If you do get this phone call, ask the caller for the web address where you can download this manual. Chances are good the caller will have a reason why that's not acceptable. Finally, remember that if someone ships you items that you didn't order, the burden is on them to retrieve them. You're legally not required to pay—either for the items or for the shipping—and you're under no obligation to return them or buy them. (ITRC)

Online Auction Scams

These are legion and exist on every e-commerce site you can think of, but there's a pattern: You are going to be asked to do something via email, whether it is a request for shipping fees or a notice informing you of a "second chance" on an eBay item narrowly missed.

Parking Ticket Scam

There are two ways these scams work: either by placing an actual paper ticket on your windshield (which is riskier as the scammer has to be physically present) or by emailing you a notice from the police department claiming that you have an unpaid parking ticket. In either case, you'll be directed to a website to pay online by credit card for your convenience.

It can be scary to receive notice from a law enforcement agency, even if you know you didn't do anything wrong, and that's exactly what the scammers are counting on. If you ever receive a ticket or an email like this, remember to verify its authenticity *before* you pay anything. The website the scammers are sending you to obviously takes your money. Unfortunately, it may not only take it one time. Once you pay, they can turn around and reuse your credit card info or even sell it. (ITRC)

Plastic Surgery Scam

There is always the possibility a scammer will get credit in your name to acquire cosmetic surgery, but did you know you can be duped into committing a crime? Common scams committed by shady doctors include sending an insurer the billing code for a covered treatment, like a deviated septum, in order to provide a client with an uncovered treatment, like a nose job. If you knowingly allow your doctor to do this, you're committing fraud.

Real Estate Scams

You're looking for a new apartment or a timeshare, or maybe you've found an incredibly sweet deal on an apartment-swapping site. What you don't know is the dream place is just that—it doesn't exist, and the person who posted the ad is accepting deposits from everyone else who saw that ad and thought the same thing as you.

Reshipping Scam

This scam involves having the victim pick up or receive packages inadvertently sent to the wrong customers, then ship them back to the company. Easy work and good pay, while actually providing a service to both the company and the customer.

Unfortunately, the people you work for aren't part of the company. They're using stolen credit cards to purchase items. Since those items have to be sent to the address that matches the credit card info on file, you're receiving the stolen goods and mailing them to the people who stole the credit card in the first place.

Guess who's going to want to talk to you? The FBI. You just trafficked stolen goods.

There is no such thing as easy money, but more importantly, there's no such thing as legitimately purchasing a product and *not* being able to have it shipped to you. If you're asked to receive any kind of items and then ship them to someone else, there's a crime being committed, and you're now a part of it.

Save Water Scam

Just like other utility or alarm system scams, this one involves either a phone call or a home visit from someone claiming to sell you a device that will reduce the cost of your monthly water bill. Whether over the phone or in person, the thief is really after access to your credit card information. Even if you do end up with a cheap faucet attachment that doesn't save you any money, that cost was small compared to the rewards the thief can reap once he has your payment information.

Tip: Never respond to cold calls offering to sell you something. If you are approached with a too-good-to-be-true offer that sounds intriguing, take the information and find the sales locations yourself.

Allowing someone to reach out to you and get your personal information is a good way to get scammed. (ITRC)

Skimmers

Keypad overlay devices, gas pump versions with Bluetooth, ATM skimmers with a pinhole camera—there are many versions. Sometimes skimmers and the hardware associated with them can be spotted (if you know what you're looking for and it's one of the skimmers you can detect, for instance by banging on the ATM machine or trying to shake the user interface module), but often it's impossible to detect a skimmer scam.

Social Media Scams (Home Invasion)

Another use of social media in crime circles involves monitoring posted photographs, for clues about where you live and what you have that's worth stealing, and status updates that provide additional information. In addition to providing a visual inventory, photographs can contain hidden information that will allow a thief to pinpoint the location of your home. Add to the mix your status updates featuring details of your day (including when you are not at home), and you might as well ring a dinner bell for this kind of crook.

Synthetic Identity Theft

This involves combining the name and address of one person, the birthdate of another, and the Social Security number of a third to create a hybrid credit file. This is a particularly efficient form of life wrecking, because it creates two victims for every criminal who benefits (the birthday donor is going to be fine).

Tax Fraud

You file your tax return by mail and receive a notice from the IRS via snail mail stating that a return has already been filed using your Social Security number. Or you submit your tax return online and then receive an alert that your return has been rejected because it contains the Social Security number of a previously filed return.

You are waiting for your refund and it doesn't arrive within the allotted time (twenty-one days for an e-filing and six weeks for a paper filing). When you call the number provided, the representative tells you that your tax refund was already sent out. You receive a deficiency notice from the IRS stating that you have significantly underreported your income, and the number that you see is far beyond any recognizable amount.

If anything like this happens to you, someone else has likely filed a tax return using your name, date of birth, and Social Security number.

Telecommunication Scams

Victims receive a call or text from their wireless or phone company directing them to a phishing site to receive a credit, discount, or prize ranging from $100 to $2,500. The monetary amounts being offered are increasing to make the scam more enticing. A fraudulent website example would be www.My(insert phone company name)900.com. Other fraudulent websites may contain words such as MyBonus, ILove, ILike, Reward, Promo, or similar words, along with a telephone company's name.

The phishing site is a replica of one of the telecommunication carrier's sites, and it requests the victim's login credentials and the last four digits of their Social Security number. Once this information is provided, thieves access the real customers' accounts, make changes to them, and may place orders for mobile phones.

Remain skeptical about the validity of unsolicited calls, emails, and text messages, especially those promising some type of remuneration for supplying account information. If you receive such an offer, verify it with the business associated with your account before supplying any information. Use the phone numbers that appear on your account statement to contact the business.

If you have fallen victim to this scam, immediately notify your telecommunication carrier and file a complaint with the IC3 at www.ic3.gov. (ITRC)

Travel Scams

You receive a letter informing you that you have a chance to cash in on a big win: free airline tickets. There have been several attempts to contact you about the tickets (you won them through a sweepstakes you have never heard of, in which you were automatically enrolled), and you're going to lose them if you don't contact the travel agency or cruise line immediately. The letter provides a toll-free number to call. You call it and there are . . . well, certain requirements. Meeting those obligations will cost you far more than the alleged free tickets.

Utility Scam

The phone rings, you receive a text, or—less likely—an email arrives. Regardless of the method of contact, you are being notified that your electricity or your gas is going to be turned off because you've reached the end of the line. Your outstanding balance is X and your account will be suspended today if you don't pay. Can't pay the entire amount? Not to worry. They'll set you up with a plan, and take a partial payment.

Vacation Property Scam

If you're planning to rent a condo, house, or similar property in another city, be sure to do your homework.

The scam happens when a thief finds a rental property online and uses the details to create his own website and listing. He'll even have bogus five-star reviews from fake renters, and it will be particularly affordable, possibly due to a one-day-only Internet sale. You book the listing and pay either by credit card or wire transfer, and you get ready to pack your bags.

Here's the problem: When the time comes and you show up for your vacation, that's not your condo. It's not just a matter of bait and switch, where the gorgeous property on the website doesn't exactly live up to the reality. In this case, the property is very real and even very beautiful . . . but you didn't rent it. There may even be another family in it that week. You now find yourself on vacation with nowhere to sleep, and your scammer is nowhere to be found.

If the person can't answer those questions accurately—or takes too long to answer, which indicates that he's also doing an online search—then that could be a red flag. It is possible that the rental agent is located in another city, but someone in his offices should have at least laid eyes on the property and be able give you an idea of the answers.

Tip: Whenever you're booking a rental property—for any reason, not just a beach getaway—there's a sneaky little trick you can use to verify the authenticity of the listing and the property. Instead of emailing, call the person on the phone, but first do an online search for other businesses in the area surrounding the property, then ask the listing agent some specific questions that you've already figured out the answers to. How far is it to the nearest beach access? Where is the nearest restaurant with a kids' menu? How far are we from an emergency room in case someone in our group gets hurt?

Virtual Kidnapping Scam

This is the newest thing and not very common yet, but it's too crazy not to get a mention. You get a call during the day, when you're not likely to be with the family member who has supposedly been abducted. There is a woman screaming in the background (meant to be your wife or daughter), and the caller says, "Meet us here." He or she demands ransom via credit card.

A variation on the theme usually involves a car accident and your loved one, who has been badly injured. The accident has happened near a gang's hangout, and they will neither call an ambulance nor tell you where to send the EMTs till you pay.

A more timely variation on this theme: Someone claiming to be with the IRS calls to inform you that your spouse has been arrested for failing to pay the taxes. However, they will be immediately released if you wire several thousand dollars to an account they designate.

Here's how you should know it's a fake: They're not in a rush to get off the phone. Real kidnappers can't get off the phone fast enough.

Wire Transfer Fraud Scam

According to a Guardian Analytics 2013 white paper, this scam begins with the hijacking of a victim's email address or it can be done via fax, at the bank branch or through its customer service. If via email, the fraudster scans the victim's communications with his relationship manager at his financial institution. Once he has a thorough understanding of the words and cadence used in their interactions, the scammer (using the victim's compromised email account) sends a request to his relationship manager explaining that he is offline and needs funds transferred as soon as possible. If the victim doesn't already have a template funds transfer letter saved in his email, the bank emails the necessary letter of authority, which the scammer receives, signs, and faxes or emails back to the institution. Because many institutions don't check signatures as carefully as they should, the funds get wired to the fraudulent account.

A different version of this scam involves fraudsters jamming the victim's cell phone, which inhibits the bank from contacting the victim in order to confirm the transaction.

A third, equally sophisticated version begins with the compromise of the victim's online banking account. The scammer accesses the account in order to view electronic images of the victim's signed checks. This time the fraudster has acquired the ability to return the executed transfer form with a forged signature.

Tip: Set up a protocol with your relationship manager. Always use some form of two-way authentication: either a code that is sent your cell phone that must be entered in order for the bank to complete the transaction, or a phone call where each side's voice is known to the other.

Three Malware Scams on the Rise

Adware

While you may think adware found on your mobile device is harmless, you could be at risk for data theft. A report from the IT security firm Avast revealed that apps in the Android app store, Google Play, could potentially infect millions of users with adware, according to the company's blog. Android is one of the most prevalent operating systems, and with this popularity comes the attention of hackers looking to exploit security flaws.

POS Malware

Retailers were a prime target for cybercriminals last year as huge data breaches affected millions of customers, making 2014 the "Year of the Data Breach." Cybercriminals infiltrated point-of-sale (POS) systems and infected them with malware designed to steal personal and financial information. In August 2014, the U.S. Computer Emergency Readiness Team (US-CERT) said several POS providers and vendors reported their clients were impacted by malware. This year, POS malware could continue to be a big problem for retailers because hackers work to customize their hacking tools specifically to exploit companies' vulnerabilities.

Since data breaches could damage a company's reputation and potentially its sales, companies must increase their security spending to improve their data breach detection, and come up with a plan in case they experience these cyberintrusions.

Ransomware

According to *Infosecurity Magazine*, in a new scheme, hackers send emails to consumers claiming their Google Chrome version is out of date and could be vulnerable. The download that comes with this supposed update is actually ransomware, and it aims to take not only sensitive files but also virtual money, such as Bitcoins. *Infosecurity Magazine* recommended that consumers avoid unsolicited emails and install malware detection tools on their devices.

APPENDIX 3

Identity Theft and the Deceased

Prevention and Victim Tips

The following steps are recommended by the Identity Theft Resource Center (ITRC) for all deaths, regardless of age. Specific requirements by the credit reporting agencies are listed below.

In Appendices 4 and 5, you'll also find information about letter forms—ITRC Letter Form LF 117-1 (Request a Credit Report for the Deceased) and ITRC Letter Form LF 117-2 (Deceased Affidavit of Fact)—that can be sent to the credit reporting agencies, creditors, and merchants when the deceased is a victim of identity theft.

It is best to notify all entities by telephone, but remember that these calls must be followed up in writing. Mail all correspondence by certified mail with return receipt requested. Keep photocopies of all correspondence, including letters that you send.

- Obtain at least twelve copies of the official death certificate when it becomes available. In some cases you will be able to use a photocopy, but some businesses will request an original death certificate. Since many death records are public, a business may require more than just a death certificate as proof.

- If there is a surviving spouse or other joint account holders, make sure to immediately notify relevant credit card companies, banks, stock brokers, loan/lien holders, and mortgage companies of the death.
- The executor or surviving spouse will need to discuss all outstanding debts and how they will be dealt with. You will need to transfer the account to another person or close it. If you close the account, ask them to list it as: "Closed. Account holder is deceased."
- Contact all credit rating agencies, credit issuers, collection agencies, and any other financial institutions that need to know of the death, using the required procedures for each one.

Include the following information in all letters:

- Name and SSN of deceased
- Last known address
- Last five years of addresses
- Date of birth
- Date of death

To speed up processing, include all requested documentation specific to that agency in the first letter.

- Request a copy of the decedent's credit report (refer to ITRC Letter Form LF 117-1 in Appendix 4). A review of each report will let you know of any active credit accounts that still need to be closed, or any pending collection notices. Be sure to ask for all contact information on accounts currently open in the name of the deceased (credit granters, collection agencies, etc.) so that you can follow through with those entities.

- Request that the report is flagged with the following alert: "Deceased. Do not issue credit. If an application is made for credit, notify the following person(s) immediately: [list the next surviving relative, executor/trustee of the estate, and/or local law enforcement agency, noting the relationship]."

Other notifications may include the following:

- Social Security Administration
- Insurance companies—auto, health, life, and so on
- Veterans Administration—if the person was a former member of the military
- Immigration Services—if the decedent was not a U.S. citizen
- Department of Motor Vehicles—if the person had a driver's license or state ID card. Also make sure that any vehicle registration papers are transferred to the new owners.
- Agencies that may be involved due to professional licenses—bar associations, medical or cosmetology licensing associations, and so on. Close any membership programs, including those for video stores, public libraries, fitness clubs, and so on.

Specific Instructions from the Credit Reporting Agencies (CRAs)

Equifax

Equifax Information Services LLC
Office of Consumer Affairs
PO Box 105139
Atlanta, GA 30348

To order a credit report:

Equifax requests that the spouse, attorney, or executor of the estate submit a written request to receive a copy of the deceased consumer's file. The request should include the following: a copy of a notarized document stating that the requestor is authorized to handle the deceased consumer's affairs (i.e., an order from a probate court or a letter of testamentary).

For requests or changes:

Equifax requests that a spouse, attorney, or executor of the estate submit a written request if they would like to place a deceased indicator on the deceased consumer's file. The written request should include a copy of the consumer's death certificate. The request should be sent to the address listed above.

Upon receipt of the death certificate, Equifax will attempt to locate a file for the deceased consumer and place a death notice on it. In addition, Equifax will place a seven-year block on the deceased consumer's file. Once Equifax's research is complete, they will send a response to the spouse, attorney, or executor of the estate.

Experian

Experian
PO Box 9701
Allen, TX 75013

To order a credit report:

A spouse can obtain a credit report by simply making the request through the regular channels—mail, phone, and Internet. The spouse is legally entitled to the report.

The executor of the estate can obtain a credit report but must write Experian with a specific request, a copy of the executor paperwork, and the death certificate.

For requests or changes:

A spouse or executor may change the file to show the person as deceased via written request. A copy of the death certificate—and, in the case of the executor, the executor's paperwork—must be included with the request.

After any changes, Experian will send an updated credit report to the spouse or executor for confirmation that a deceased statement has been added to the credit report. This is important as executors and spouses can request other types of "changes" that Experian may not be able to honor.

If identity theft is a stated concern, Experian will add a security alert after the file has been changed to reflect that the person is deceased.

If there are additional concerns, Experian will add a general statement to the file at the direction of the spouse/executor. The spouse/executor must state specifically what they want the general statement to say, such as "Do not issue credit."

TransUnion

TransUnion
PO Box 2000
Chester, PA 19022-2000

To order a credit report:

TransUnion requires proof of a power of attorney, executor of estate, conservatorship, or other legal document giving the requestor the legal right to obtain a copy of the decedent's credit file.

If the requestor was married to the deceased and the address for which the credit file is being mailed to is contained on the decedent's credit file, then TransUnion will mail a credit file to the surviving spouse.

If the deceased is a minor child of the requestor, TransUnion will mail a credit file to the parent upon receipt of a copy of the birth certificate or death certificate naming the parent as requestor.

For requests or changes:

TransUnion will accept a request to place a temporary deceased alert on the credit file of a deceased individual from any consumer who makes such a request and identifies themselves as having a right to do so.

The requestor's phone number is added to the temporary, three-month alert. Upon receipt of a verifiable death certificate, TransUnion will entirely suppress the decedent's credit file and note it as belonging to a deceased consumer.

TransUnion will not mail out a copy of its contents without the requirements mentioned above.

If you suspect fraud, TransUnion suggests that you call their fraud unit at 800-680-7289. They will place the temporary alert and advise the requestor of what needs to be sent to suppress the credit file and to disclose a copy of its contents. Requests can also be emailed to fvad@transunion.com.

Take the following steps if you (the surviving spouse or estate executor) suspect that someone is fraudulently using the information of a deceased person:

- Request a copy of the decedent's credit report (refer to ITRC Letter Form LF 117-1, Appendix 4), then place a flag on the account stating "deceased alert" on the report, as outlined above.
- Notify the police in the decedent's jurisdiction if you have evidence of fraud (collection notice, bills, or credit report). A report of a suspicion of identity theft is most effective when backed with concrete evidence.
- Notify any creditor, collection agency, credit issuer, or utility company that the person is deceased and give the

date of death by using ITRC Letter Form LF 117-2 (Appendix 5). Be sure to include a copy of the death certificate. Request an immediate investigation and ask that they contact you with the results. Insist on letters of clearance, which you should keep with the other estate papers.

APPENDIX 4

Request a Credit Report
for the Deceased

ITRC Letter Form 117-1

ITRC Letter Form 117-1 is to be sent to the three credit reporting agencies (CRAs) to request the information on somebody who is deceased. NOTE: Only the surviving spouse, someone with power of attorney for the deceased, or the executor of the estate may request this information.

Equifax:
Equifax Information Services LLC
Office of Consumer Affairs
PO Box 105139
Atlanta, GA 30348

Experian:
PO Box 4500
Allen, TX 75013

TransUnion:
PO Box 2000
Chester, PA 19022

A template is available for download at www.idtheftcenter.org /images/documents/LF-117-1.pdf.

This letter form should not be used in lieu of legal advice. Any requests to reproduce this material, other than by individual victims for their own use, should be directed to itrc@idtheftcenter .org. ITRC thanks the CRAs for providing material for this guide.

APPENDIX 5
Deceased Affidavit of Fact

ITRC Letter Form 117-2

ITRC Letter Form 117-2 is an affidavit of fact to be sent to the CRAs, creditors, and/or merchants if identity theft of a deceased person has occurred.

A template is available for download at www.idtheftcenter.org /images/documents/LF-117-2.pdf.

Acknowledgments

This book has been a long time in the making—and even longer in the talking about. To the many friends and family along the way who encouraged me to "write a book," I am so very grateful. And to my dear, late friend Judy who said a few months before she passed, "Write the damn thing already!" I did it!

Jim Levine of the Levine Greenberg Rostan Literary Agency provided crucial guidance when I most needed it. His clear-eyed presence in the creative process kept the project on track and on message. Needless to say without him, we wouldn't have gotten here.

PublicAffairs was the clear choice for me after we met with Publisher Clive Priddle, Lisa Kauffman, Lindsay Fradkoff, Jaime Leifer, and of course my editor Benjamin Adams, whose acumen, wit, enthusiasm, and collaborative spirit are in evidence throughout this book. Ben provided timely suggestions, and was an excellent guide, never shy about saying when I needed to ease up and stop scaring readers to death and when I needed to scare them even more. He was an invaluable asset in the process of getting this book finished, and it would be a different project had he not been a part of it.

None of our work would have mattered were it not for the dauntless and relentless efforts of the whole team at PublicAffairs. Many thanks in particular to Chris Juby and Debbie Masi.

When it came to making sure no one in America slept without becoming first aware of this book, the honor falls to Miss Lelani Clark, my fearless publicity director, co-conspirator and trusted colleague. She was already promoting *Swiped* before the ink was dry on our contract. Thanks also to Travis Taylor.

Special thanks to Virginia Long, former Associate Justice of the New Jersey Supreme Court and my mentor and predecessor at the New Jersey Division of Consumer Affairs who brought me into the world of consumer protection, believed in me, and put me on the fascinating and winding path that has culminated with the writing of this book.

To my writing partner, collaborator, friend, conscience, pseudo-shrink, confidante, sounding board, future radio side-kick, brand strategist, and fellow neurotic, Beau Friedlander, thank you from the bottom of my heart for your indomitable spirit, your tireless work, and for incessantly hammering me on a daily basis to buckle down and just do it! Actually IRLY (you know what I am talking about).

To my colleagues at Credit.com (in particular Ian Cohen, Michael Schreiber, Kali Geldis, and Melissa Heltzel), who make sure that my articles are published and edited every week on a huge content distribution network, and the wonderful people at IDT911 (Matt Cullina, Sean Daly, Brian Chertok, Scott Frazee, and Debbie Sutherland), many thanks. A special shout-out to Brian Huntley, who helped me figure out the Three Ms for enterprise; Eduard Goodman, who has always been there to answer any legal question I had; and Deena Coffman who enthusiastically and promptly responded to urgent emails while I was in the heat of composition.

A special thanks to everyone at the IDT911 Resolution Center who do so much to help people and have provided scores of heart-wrenching stories for us to share here and in our articles every week. Victor Searcy, Vickie Volkert, and Brett Montgomery, thank you so much for helping to make sure this book accurately recounted everything we do.

My thanks to Eva Casey Velasquez of the Identity Theft Resource Center, who provided invaluable interviews and also gave me permission to use the ITRC's list of common scams, which are found in Appendix 2 (and indicated with a parenthetical credit). The Philip and Janice Levin Foundation is proud to be a major sponsor of all the good works done by the ITRC.

Thanks to Ann Cavoukian, former Information and Privacy Commissioner for Ontario and now Executive Director of the Privacy and Big Data Institute at Ryerson University, Pam Dixon of the World Privacy Forum, Beth Givens of the Privacy Rights Clearing House, Joanne McNabb of the California Office of the Attorney General, Larry Ponemon of the Ponemon Institute, and Susan Grant of the Consumer Federation of America—whom we either quote or cite—for their assistance and inspiration.

My thanks to my friends and colleagues Bob Sullivan, Herb Weisbaum, Byron Acohido, Gerri Detweiler, Christine DiGangi, and Brian Krebs for their support and/or inspiration over the years.

Thanks to David Fisher who helped create the historical section, my pal Joe (he prefers to be referenced as "Machiavelli"), who not only helped convince me that it was time to write, but introduced me to Beau and my wife. And thanks to Tony and Harris, who had told me for years I should write the Cybergeddon book that (although within the realm of possibility) would have mentally scarred my readers for decades.

Finally, endless gratitude and appreciation go to the loves of my life, Heather and Jayger Wilde. Without them, this book would not exist, and quite possibly neither would I. I cannot thank you both enough for completely understanding, supporting, and loving me through those many nights and weekends I spent camped out in my office; the countless (and seemingly endless) hours I lived on the phone with Beau; and most of all, for giving me encouragement when my creative juices turned to dust. I will always love you.

I would love to name everyone with whom I have ever worked, but this is not the Academy Awards and I don't want to be played off the stage.

P.S. One final word of appreciation to Adam Levine: I can't begin to count the number media gigs (and tables at really good restaurants) I booked because people thought I was you. You can imagine their disappointment when I actually showed up.

Index

ADAM LEVIN is a consumer advocate with more than thirty years' experience in personal finance, privacy, real estate, and government service. A former director of the New Jersey Division of Consumer Affairs, Levin is chairman and founder of Identity Theft 911, and chairman and cofounder of Credit.com, and he serves as a spokesperson for both companies. He writes weekly columns for *Huffington Post* and ABCNews.com, and has appeared on *Fox News, Fox Business News, Good Morning America, Fox and Friends, CBS Evening News, ABC World News Tonight,* and scores of radio stations throughout the country. He lives in New York City.

PublicAffairs is a publishing house founded in 1997. It is a tribute to the standards, values, and flair of three persons who have served as mentors to countless reporters, writers, editors, and book people of all kinds, including me.

I. F. STONE, proprietor of *I. F. Stone's Weekly*, combined a commitment to the First Amendment with entrepreneurial zeal and reporting skill and became one of the great independent journalists in American history. At the age of eighty, Izzy published *The Trial of Socrates*, which was a national bestseller. He wrote the book after he taught himself ancient Greek.

BENJAMIN C. BRADLEE was for nearly thirty years the charismatic editorial leader of *The Washington Post*. It was Ben who gave the *Post* the range and courage to pursue such historic issues as Watergate. He supported his reporters with a tenacity that made them fearless and it is no accident that so many became authors of influential, best-selling books.

ROBERT L. BERNSTEIN, the chief executive of Random House for more than a quarter century, guided one of the nation's premier publishing houses. Bob was personally responsible for many books of political dissent and argument that challenged tyranny around the globe. He is also the founder and longtime chair of Human Rights Watch, one of the most respected human rights organizations in the world.

·   ·   ·

For fifty years, the banner of Public Affairs Press was carried by its owner Morris B. Schnapper, who published Gandhi, Nasser, Toynbee, Truman, and about 1,500 other authors. In 1983, Schnapper was described by *The Washington Post* as "a redoubtable gadfly." His legacy will endure in the books to come.

Peter Osnos, *Founder and Editor-at-Large*